Experiencing and Enjoying Christ to Abound in the Work of Christ according to His Full Ministry of Three Stages— Incarnation, Inclusion, and Intensification

The Holy Word for Morning Revival

Witness Lee

Living Stream Ministry
Anaheim, CA • www.lsm.org

First Edition, June 2008.

ISBN 978-0-7363-3781-6

Published by

Living Stream Ministry
2431 W. La Palma Ave., Anaheim, CA 92801 U.S.A.
P. O. Box 2121, Anaheim, CA 92814 U.S.A.

Printed in the United States of America

08 09 10 11 12 / 7 6 5 4 3 2 1

Contents

Preface

1. This book is intended as an aid to believers in developing a daily time of morning revival with the Lord in His word. At the same time, it provides a limited review of the Memorial Day weekend conference held in Dallas, Texas, May 23-26, 2008. Through intimate contact with the Lord in His word, the believers can be constituted with life and truth and thereby equipped to prophesy in the meetings of the church unto the building up of the Body of Christ.

2. The entire content of this book is taken primarily from the published conference outlines, the text and footnotes of the Recovery Version of the Bible, selections from the writings of Witness Lee and Watchman Nee, and *Hymns,* all of which are published by Living Stream Ministry.

3. The book is divided into weeks. One conference message is covered per week. Each week presents first the message outline, followed by six daily portions, a hymn, and then some space for writing. The message outline has been divided into days, corresponding to the six daily portions. Each daily portion covers certain points and begins with a section entitled "Morning Nourishment." This section contains selected verses and a short reading that can provide rich spiritual nourishment through intimate fellowship with the Lord. The "Morning Nourishment" is followed by a section entitled "Today's Reading," a longer portion of ministry related to the day's main points. Each day's portion concludes with a short list of references for further reading and some space for the saints to make notes concerning their spiritual inspiration, enlightenment, and enjoyment to serve as a reminder of what they have received of the Lord that day.

4. The space provided at the end of each week is for composing a short prophecy. This prophecy can be composed by considering all of our daily notes, the "harvest" of our inspirations during the week, and preparing a main point

with some sub-points to be spoken in the church meetings for the organic building up of the Body of Christ.

5. Following the last week in this volume, we have provided
reading schedules for both the Old and New Testaments
in the Recovery Version with footnotes. These schedules
are arranged so that one can read through both the Old
and New Testaments of the Recovery Version with footnotes in two years.

6. As a practical aid to the saints' feeding on the Word
throughout the day, we have provided verse cards at the
end of the volume, which correspond to each day's scripture reading. These may be removed and carried along
as a source of spiritual enlightenment and nourishment
in the saints' daily lives.

7. The conference message outlines were compiled by Living
Stream Ministry from the writings of Witness Lee and
Watchman Nee. The outlines, footnotes, and references
in the Recovery Version of the Bible are by Witness Lee.
All of the other references cited in this publication are
from the published ministry of Witness Lee and Watchman Nee.

Memorial Day Weekend Conference
(May 23-26, 2008)

General Subject:

Experiencing and Enjoying Christ to Abound in the Work of Christ according to His Full Ministry of Three Stages—Incarnation, Inclusion, and Intensification

Banners:

We need to experience and enjoy Christ
to abound in the work of Christ
according to His full ministry of three stages—
incarnation, inclusion, and intensification.

The seven Spirits as the seven eyes of Christ,
the Lamb, infuse all that the Lamb is
into our being so that we may be transformed
into His image for God's building.

Christ as the sevenfold intensified Spirit is working
to produce the overcomers by bringing them
out of the degradation of the church
back to the enjoyment of Himself
for the finalization of God's New Testament economy.

Under the burning of the seven Spirits
as the seven lamps of fire, the churches
as golden lampstands will consummate in
the New Jerusalem as the universal,
eternal golden lampstand.

Experiencing, Enjoying, and Ministering Christ according to the Three Divine and Mystical Stages of His Full Ministry

Scripture Reading: John 1:14; 1 Cor. 15:45b; Rev. 4:5; 5:6; Psa. 45

Day 1

I. **We need to experience and enjoy Christ according to the three stages of His full ministry, and we need to abound in the threefold work of the ministry to build up the Body of Christ (Phil. 3:8; Eph. 4:11-12; 1 Cor. 3:12; 15:58; 16:10; Phil. 1:22-25; 2:30; 2 Cor. 5:18-20; 6:1):**

A. The first stage is the stage of His incarnation—the stage of Christ as a man in the flesh; the work of the ministry in this stage produces redeemed people (Matt. 14:19, 23; John 1:14; 5:30; 7:18; 10:30; 14:30b; Psa. 109:4b; Rom. 3:24-25).

B. The second stage is the stage of His inclusion—the stage of Christ as the life-giving Spirit; the work of the ministry in this stage produced the church and produces the churches (1 Cor. 15:45b; John 20:22; Phil. 1:19; Acts 20:28).

C. The third stage is the stage of His intensification—the stage of Christ as the sevenfold intensified Spirit; the work of the ministry in this stage produces the overcomers as today's Zion (Rev. 1:4; 4:5; 5:6; 3:1; 2:7, 17; 3:20; 19:7-9).

Day 2

II. **Psalm 45 presents a complete view, a full picture, of the all-inclusive Christ in His beauty according to His full ministry of three divine and mystical stages—incarnation (in the Gospels—vv. 1-8), inclusion (in the Epistles—vv. 9-15), and intensification (in Revelation—vv. 16-17):**

A. Psalm 45, the highest and greatest of all the psalms, is one of the psalms of the sons of Korah, a song of love according to the melody of lilies:

1. The great work of God is to restore the

desolated building of God and to recover "the sons of Korah" by transforming rebellious ones, through His unlimited mercy and grace, into Christ's overcomers to make them the constituents of His bride, His overcoming queen (Num. 16:1-3; Psa. 42, title; 106:16; 1 Chron. 6:33-37; Psa. 88, title; Rev. 19:7-9).

2. If we are those who affectionately love the Lord, we eventually become His love, His favorite (S. S. 1:1-4, 14-15; 2:4).

3. A lily denotes a pure, simple, single life of trusting in God (vv. 1-2; Matt. 6:28-29; cf. 1 Kings 7:17-19).

B. If we have an affectionate love for the Lord Jesus, our tongue will be the pen of a ready writer, ready to write our love for Him and our praise to Him with our experience and enjoyment of Him according to all that He is in His full ministry (Psa. 45:1; Matt. 12:34b; Isa. 6:5-7; 2 Cor. 3:3, 6).

Day 3 C. Psalm 45 praises Christ the King as unveiled in the four Gospels (vv. 1-8):

1. The psalmist praises Christ the King in His fairness; Christ is fairer than the sons of men (vv. 1-2; cf. 27:4; S. S. 5:9-16):

   a. Grace is poured upon Christ's lips (Luke 4:17-22; cf. Eph. 4:29-30).

   b. Because the man Jesus is fair, sweet, and full of grace, God has been moved to bless Him forever (Rom. 9:5).

2. The psalmist praises Christ the King in His victory (Psa. 45:3-5):

   a. In the eyes of Satan and his fallen angels, Christ is the mighty One who has girded His sword upon His thigh, the One with majesty and splendor as signs of His victory (v. 3).

   b. In His splendor Christ rides on victoriously because of truth, meekness, and righteousness; regardless of what the situation is on earth, regardless of what the nations are doing, Christ is riding on triumphantly, prosperously; from the day of His ascension, He began to ride on, and He will continue to ride until He comes back in victory (v. 4a; Acts 5:31; Rev. 6:2; 19:11-16).

    c. His right hand performs awesome deeds; Christ's awesome deeds include His crucifixion, resurrection, and ascension; everything that the Lord Jesus does, whether great or small, is awesome (Psa. 45:4b).

    d. His arrows are sharp in the heart of His enemies, and the peoples fall under Him (v. 5; cf. Rev. 6:2).

Day 4

3. The psalmist praises Christ the King in His kingdom (Psa. 45:6-7):

    a. As God, Christ's throne is forever and ever, and the scepter of uprightness is the scepter of His kingdom (v. 6; Heb. 1:8).

    b. As the King, Christ has loved righteousness and hated wickedness, and God the Father has anointed Christ with the oil of gladness above His companions (Psa. 45:7; Heb. 1:9).

4. The psalmist praises Christ the King in the sweetness of His virtues (Psa. 45:8; cf. 1 Pet. 2:9):

    a. All His garments smell of myrrh and aloes and of cassia (Psa. 45:8a):

      (1) Garments signify Christ's deeds and virtues, myrrh and aloes signify the sweetness of His death, and cassia signifies the fragrance and repelling power of Christ's resurrection.

      (2) The way to experience Christ in His crucifixion by the power of His

resurrection is by the Spirit Himself
who is in our spirit (cf. S. S. 2:8-14;
Rom. 8:16; Phil. 3:10).

b. From palaces of ivory, harpstrings have
made Him glad (Psa. 45:8b):

(1) Palaces signify local churches, ivory
signifies the resurrection life of
Christ (John 19:36; cf. S. S. 7:4; 4:4;
1 Kings 10:18), and harpstrings signify praises.

(2) The local churches are beautiful in
the eyes of the Lord and are His
expression, and they are built with
the resurrection life of Christ; from the
local churches come the praises that
make Him glad.

Day 5   D. Psalm 45 praises Christ the King in praising
the queen, the church, His wife, as revealed in
the Epistles (vv. 9-15):

1. The queen typifies the church, especially the
overcomers, as the unique wife of Christ,
and the honorable women around the queen
signify Christ's overcoming guests; this
indicates that the bride of Christ is actually
a group of overcomers (vv. 9-10):

a. The daughters of kings signify the believers of Christ in their royalty.

b. The king's most prized women signify the
believers of Christ in their honor and
majesty.

2. The king desires the queen's beauty; the
queen's beauty signifies the virtues of
Christ expressed through the church (v. 11):

a. The beauty of the bride comes from the
Christ who is wrought into the church
and who is then expressed through the
church (Eph. 1:18-23; 3:16-21; 5:25-27).

b. Our only beauty is the shining out of
Christ from within us; what Christ

Day 6

appreciates in us is the expression of Himself (Phil. 1:20; 2:15-16; Isa. 60:1, 5; cf. Exo. 28:2).

3. In Psalm 45 the queen has two garments:
   a. The first garment is the gold of Ophir, the woven work inwrought with gold (vv. 9b, 13b):
      (1) This garment corresponds to Christ as our objective righteousness, which is for our salvation (Luke 15:22; 1 Cor. 1:30; Isa. 61:10).
      (2) The queen's being covered with gold signifies the church's appearing in the divine nature (Psa. 45:9b; 2 Pet. 1:4).
      (3) The garment of woven work inwrought with gold signifies that the Christ who has been dealt with through death and resurrection is the righteousness of the church to meet the righteous requirement of God for her to be justified by God (Gal. 2:16; Rom. 3:26).
   b. The second garment is the embroidered clothing (Psa. 45:14a):
      (1) This garment corresponds to Christ lived out of us as our subjective righteousnesses, which are for our victory (Rev. 19:8).
      (2) As our subjective righteousnesses, Christ is the One dwelling in us to live for us a life that is always acceptable to God (Phil. 3:9; Matt. 5:6, 20; Rom. 8:4; cf. Psa. 23:3).
      (3) The garment of embroidered clothing signifies that the church will be led to Christ, clothed with the righteousnesses of the saints to meet the requirement of Christ for their marriage (Rev. 19:8; cf. Matt. 22:11-14).

    4. The king's daughter is all glorious within the royal abode, and the virgins will enter the king's palace (Psa. 45:13a, 14-15):

       a. The king's daughter is the queen, signifying the church, and her being glorious within the royal abode signifies the glorious church taking Christ as her royal abode (v. 13a; John 15:4a).

       b. We take Christ as our abode, we become His abode, and this mutual abode eventually becomes the palace, which signifies the New Jerusalem (14:23; 15:5; Psa. 45:15b; Rev. 21:3, 22).

E. Psalm 45 praises Christ the King in praising His sons, the overcomers as the princes, as seen in Revelation (Psa. 45:16-17):

    1. "In the place of Your fathers will be Your sons; / You will make them princes in all the earth" (v. 16):

       a. Here *fathers* signifies Christ's forefathers in the flesh, *sons* signifies the overcomers of Christ as His descendants, and *princes* signifies the overcomers of Christ as His co-kings, who will reign with Christ over the nations (Rev. 2:26-27; 20:4, 6).

       b. Only Christ the King reigning on the earth with the overcomers as His helpers in the kingship can solve the problems of today's world (Isa. 42:1-4; Hag. 2:7a).

    2. Christ's name will be remembered in all generations through the overcoming saints, and Christ will be praised by the nations through His overcoming and co-reigning saints (Psa. 45:17).

Morning Nourishment

John
1:14

And the Word became flesh and tabernacled among us (and we beheld His glory, glory as of the only Begotten from the Father), full of grace and reality.

1 Cor.
15:45

So also it is written, "The first man, Adam, became a living soul"; the last Adam *became* a life-giving Spirit.

Rev.
5:6

And I saw in the midst of the throne and of the four living creatures and in the midst of the elders a Lamb standing as having *just* been slain, having seven horns and seven eyes, which are the seven Spirits of God sent forth into all the earth.

2:7

He who has an ear, let him hear what the Spirit says to the churches. To him who overcomes, to him I will give to eat of the tree of life, which is in the Paradise of God.

[We need to] see the three stages, the three sections, of Christ: incarnation—the stage of Christ in the flesh; inclusion—the stage of Christ as the life-giving Spirit; and intensification—the stage of Christ as the sevenfold intensified life-giving Spirit. These three stages are the three sections of Christ's history. This means that Christ's history is divided into the section of His incarnation, the section of His inclusion, and the section of His intensification. Therefore we emphasize these three words—*incarnation, inclusion,* and *intensification*—and stress the facts that incarnation produces redeemed people, that inclusion produces the churches, and that intensification produces the overcomers to build up the Body, which consummates in the New Jerusalem as the unique goal of God's economy. This is the revelation in the New Testament. (*Incarnation, Inclusion, and Intensification,* p. 21)

Today's Reading

We need to do a work of three sections. We should not only be able to do the work of the first section, the section of incarnation, to produce redeemed people, but we should also be able to do a work that can serve the purpose of the second section, the section of inclusion, to produce churches. Furthermore, we should be able to do a work to build up the Body of Christ consummating the

New Jerusalem. This is the work of the stage of intensification.

The first stage—incarnation—is in the physical realm for the accomplishment of judicial redemption, which is a physical matter. The second stage—inclusion—is divine and mystical. In the third stage—intensification—there will be a maturing and a ripening in the divine and mystical realm, and the Body will be built up to consummate the New Jerusalem.

If we are carrying out this threefold work, we will work not only to produce redeemed ones and work to establish churches but will also work to build up the Body consummating the New Jerusalem.

I would ask the co-workers to consider what kind of work they have done in the past and ask themselves if they have been doing a work of three sections. Regarding my own work I can say that the work which I did in mainland China was mainly to produce redeemed people. Only a small part of my work there was for the producing of churches. This indicates that my work in China was mainly a work in the first stage. However, when I came to Taiwan, I began to do a work in the stage of inclusion, and many churches were raised up. Now I am burdened to carry out a work in the stage of intensification. Therefore, I pray to the Lord, saying, "Lord, I am endeavoring to do my best to be an overcomer for the building up of Your Body to consummate the New Jerusalem."

The church should issue in the Body of Christ, but regrettably, as the Epistles reveal, the church gradually became degraded, even at Paul's time. Because of this degradation, the compound life-giving Spirit was intensified sevenfold to become the sevenfold intensified Spirit (Rev. 1:4; 5:6). This sevenfold intensified Spirit is for the overcoming of the degradation of the church and the producing of the overcomers so that the Body of Christ can be built up in a practical way to consummate the New Jerusalem, which is the unique and eternal goal of God's heart's desire. (*Incarnation, Inclusion, and Intensification,* pp. 20-21, 11)

Further Reading: Incarnation, Inclusion, and Intensification, chs. 1-2

Enlightenment and inspiration: _____

_____

_____

_____

Morning Nourishment

Psa. To the choir director: according to Shoshannim. Of
45 (title) the sons of Korah. A Maschil; a song of love.
   1 My heart overflows with a good matter; I speak
      what I have composed concerning the King. My
      tongue is the pen of a ready writer.

Psalm 45 presents a complete view, a full picture, of Christ's beauty, which is in Christ Himself (vv. 1-8), as unveiled in the four Gospels; in the church, His wife (vv. 9-15), as revealed in the Epistles; and in all His sons, the overcomers as the princes (vv. 16-17), as seen in Revelation. (Psa. 45:16, footnote 1)

Psalm 45 [is] the highest and the greatest of the one hundred fifty psalms. To enter into the significance of such a psalm is not easy. All seventeen verses of Psalm 45 are quite common, but the way this psalm presents Christ is very peculiar.

The title of this psalm tells us that it is a song of love. The word *love* in the title refers not to a father's love for his son but to the love between a male and a female. This is indicated by the fact that the Hebrew word for love here is in the feminine gender. Thus, the love in Psalm 45 is a feminine love.

In order to understand this psalm, we need to turn to the particular book in the Bible which is concerned with love—the Song of Songs. Psalm 45 is a psalm of love, and Song of Songs is a book of love. In that book the word love is used in both the masculine and the feminine gender....The Lord Jesus is called "the Beloved"; however, the Hebrew word is simply the word for love in the masculine gender. Likewise, when the Lord calls His seeker "My love," the Hebrew word for love is in the feminine gender. Moreover, Psalm 45:2a says, "You are fairer than the sons of men." This is similar to Song of Songs 5:10, where the seeker speaks of her beloved as "distinguished among ten thousand." This is a further indication that Song of Songs helps us to understand Psalm 45. (*Life-study of the Psalms,* pp. 247-248)

Today's Reading

[The title of Psalm 45] calls it "a song of love."...It is the love between us and the Lord. This love makes us His love....If we are those who love the Lord, we eventually become His love, His favorite. Just as He is our love, so we become His love.

The subject of this psalm is love, and the tune, the melody, is called *Shoshannim,* meaning *lilies.* Here both love and lilies refer to the saints. Every lover of the Lord Jesus is feminine and is also a lily. A lily denotes a pure, simple, single life of trusting in God. Our love for the Lord Jesus should be a love full of affection. We should not only have a life of purity and simplicity as signified by the lily, but we should always have an affectionate feeling toward the Lord. According to Psalm 45, we all need to have a pure life with an affectionate love for the Lord.

John Nelson Darby, who lived to be eighty-four and never married, had such a love full of affection. One night in his old age, he was staying alone in a hotel, and at bedtime he said, "Lord, I still love You." When I read about this, I was deeply touched, desiring to have such an affectionate love for the Lord Jesus. Now I can testify that, as an elderly person, I love Him much more than I did when I was young. Recently I had a time of intimate, affectionate prayer to the Lord regarding a certain matter, and in my prayer I told Him, "Lord Jesus, I love You." As I was praying, I fell in love with the Lord Jesus once again.

Verse 1...says that the psalmist's heart overflows....For the psalmist's tongue to be the pen of a ready writer means that the psalmist does not need to write a draft of what will be spoken concerning the King. Real love for the King makes a draft unnecessary. Regarding many things we may need to write a draft, but to write a draft of what we want to say to someone we love would be altogether mechanical; it would not be real. If we have an affectionate love for the Lord Jesus, we will have the tongue of a ready writer. Instead of needing to write a draft, we will be ready to write our love and our praise. (*Life-study of the Psalms,* pp. 250-251)

Further Reading: Life-study of the Psalms, msgs. 19-20; *Christ and the Church Revealed and Typified in the Psalms,* ch. 16

Enlightenment and inspiration: _____

_____

_____

_____

Morning Nourishment

Psa. You are fairer than the sons of men; grace is poured
45:2-5 upon Your lips; therefore God has blessed You forever. Gird Your sword upon Your thigh, O mighty
One, *in* Your majesty and Your splendor. And in
Your splendor ride on victoriously because of
truth and meekness *and* righteousness; and let
Your right hand teach You awesome deeds. Your
arrows are sharp: the peoples fall under You; *the
arrows* are in the heart of the King's enemies.

The first eight verses of Psalm 45...are on the praise of Christ
as the King from four directions: His fairness, His victory, His
kingdom, and His virtues. First, the psalmist praises the King in
His fairness (v. 2a), in His handsomeness. Christ is truly fair; He
is really handsome. Christ's fairness, however, is balanced by His
victory (vv. 3-5)....Fairness and victory are a pair.

A second pair in this psalm involves Christ's kingdom (Psa.
45:6-7) and His virtues (v. 8). The kingdom is higher than the victory. Christ's kingdom is the issue of His victory. If there were no
victory, there would be no kingdom. Victory produces the kingdom. Because Christ has won the victory, the kingdom belongs
to Him. The matter of His kingdom, however, is balanced by
the sweetness of His virtues. Therefore, in the praise of Christ
as the King in Psalm 45, there are two balanced pairs: fairness and victory, kingdom and virtues. (*Life-study of the Psalms,*
pp. 249-250)

Today's Reading

[In Psalm 45:2] the psalmist praises the King (signifying
Christ) in His fairness. When the Lord Jesus comes to us, He
comes first in the aspect of His fairness. This is why, when we
preach the gospel, we need to preach mainly Christ's fairness,
telling others how good and loving Christ is. We may say that this
kind of gospel preaching is a "hook" with a tasty "bait." Everyone
who believes in the Lord Jesus and loves Him has been "hooked"
by Him. Blessed are they who have been hooked by Christ!

Now the One who has come to us in His fairness, the One who has caught us and who loves us, wants us to love Him in return. We need to love Him and even become His love. This is the issue of Christ's showing us His fairness and of our enjoyment of Christ in His fairness.

According to verse 2,...because the man Jesus is fair, sweet, and full of grace, God has been moved to bless Him forever. Thus, Romans 9:5 speaks of Christ as "God...blessed forever."

In Psalm 45:3-5 we have the psalmist's praising the King in His victory. Adam and all his descendants, including us, have been defeated. Only Christ is the Victor. The Gospels reveal that He has overcome everything and has gained the victory.

In the eyes of Satan and of all the fallen angels, Christ is the mighty One who has girded His sword upon His thigh, the One with majesty and splendor [v. 3]. Both His majesty and His splendor are signs of His victory.

Splendor [in verse 4a] is the expression of glory. While Christ was on earth, the only time He showed His splendor was when He was transfigured on the mountain (Matt. 17:1-2). But after His resurrection and ascension, He showed Himself in His splendor and majesty to Paul (Acts 26:13-15) and to John (Rev. 1:9-20).

[In Psalm 45:4b] we understand the word *teach* to mean perform. Christ has performed many awesome deeds, including His crucifixion, resurrection, and ascension. The most awesome deed performed by Christ was His crucifixion. Christ's crucifixion was a great event that threatened Satan, the demons, and the fallen angels, the powers of darkness in the air. The cross of Christ is the most awesome thing in the universe. Whereas we appreciate the cross, Satan flees from it.

Psalm 45:5 goes on to say that the King's arrows are sharp and that the peoples fall under Him. His arrows are in the heart of His enemies. (*Life-study of the Psalms,* pp. 251-254)

Further Reading: Christ and the Church Revealed and Typified in the Psalms, ch. 7

Enlightenment and inspiration: _____

_____
_____
_____

Morning Nourishment

Psa. Your throne, O God, is forever and ever; the scepter
45:6-8 of uprightness is the scepter of Your kingdom. You
have loved righteousness and hated wickedness;
therefore God, Your God, has anointed You with the
oil of gladness above Your companions. All Your
garments *smell* of myrrh and aloes, of cassia; from
palaces of ivory, harpstrings have made You glad.

In Psalm 45:6 and 7 the psalmist praises the King in His kingdom. We have pointed out that the kingdom is the issue of the victory. Hence, before one can be a king, he must first be a victor.
According to the ancient custom, the person who was victorious
over the enemies became the king.

As God, Christ's throne is forever and ever (v. 6a; Heb. 1:8a)....
The scepter [Psa. 45:6b] signifies authority. The authority of
many of today's high officials is not upright, but Christ's authority
is altogether upright.

As the King Christ has loved righteousness and hated wickedness (v. 7a; Heb. 1:9a). The more righteous we are, the more
authority we have. However, the more we are involved with wickedness, the more we lose our authority.

The oil of gladness [Psa. 45:7b] signifies the Spirit of God, and
the companions signify the believers of Christ. God the Father
has anointed Christ with the Holy Spirit above all His companions, above all His believers. This indicates that Christ's authority
and kingdom are altogether a spiritual matter. He has been
anointed for the purpose of the kingdom. Christ's authority,
throne, scepter, and everything related to the kingdom are under
the anointing of the Spirit and therefore are spiritual. (*Life-study
of the Psalms,* pp. 254-255)

Today's Reading

In Psalm 45:8 the psalmist praises the King in the sweetness
of His virtues. Regarding Christ's virtues, 1 Peter 2:9 speaks of
telling out "the virtues of Him who has called you out of darkness
into His marvelous light." When we preach the gospel, we tell

others what Christ has done for us and what He is doing for us today. To preach the gospel is actually to tell forth the many virtues of Christ, including His love, kindness, and forgiveness.

Christ's virtues are the expression of the divine attributes. For instance, with God the Father the divine love is an attribute of the Godhead. This attribute is in the divine life. As Christ lives out the divine life, He lives out the divine attribute of love. In Christ's living there is the virtue of love, and this virtue is the expression of the divine attribute of love. As we preach the gospel, we should tell others about the attributes of God expressed in the virtues of Christ.

[Psalm 45:8a speaks of the King's garments.] A person's garments signify the virtues of that person, because the way we dress is an expression of the kind of person we are and indicates our attitude and demeanor. For this reason, we can know something about a person by the way he dresses. Actually, as human beings we are under two kinds of covering—our clothing and dwelling place, both of which express what kind of person we are. Here in Psalm 45 garments signify Christ's virtues; myrrh and aloes signify the sweetness of Christ's death; and cassia signifies the fragrance of Christ's resurrection.

In verse 8b palaces signify local churches; ivory signifies the resurrection life of Christ (John 19:36); and harpstrings signify praises. The local churches, which are beautiful in the eyes of the Lord and which are His expression, are built with the resurrection life of Christ, and from the local churches are the praises that make Him glad. As we praise the Lord, we need to appreciate what He is in His virtues and what He has done to produce the church to be His expression. In a very real sense, Christ's garments, His virtues, have produced the church as His expression, and both His garments and the church are full of sweetness. May we all learn to praise Him more, especially at the Lord's table. (*Life-study of the Psalms*, pp. 255-256)

Further Reading: Life-study of the Psalms, msg. 20; Christ and the Church Revealed and Typified in the Psalms, ch. 7

Enlightenment and inspiration: _____
_____
_____
_____

Morning Nourishment

Psa. The daughters of kings are among Your most prized;
45:9-12 the queen stands at Your right hand in the gold of
Ophir. Hear, O daughter, and see; and incline your
ear; and forget your people and your father's house;
thus the King will desire your beauty. Because He is
your Lord, worship Him. And the daughter of Tyre
will come with a gift; the rich among the people will
entreat your favor.

The praise in Psalm 45 is marvelous. It praises Christ not only
concerning the things that are of Him directly—His fairness, victory, majesty, kingdom, and sweetness—but also concerning the
things that are of Him indirectly through His church and His overcomers. Since the overcomers are Christ's members, whatever is of
them directly is of Him indirectly and is His glory. Thus, the fairness of Christ in this psalm is of two layers: the first layer, the
layer that is of Himself directly, and the second layer, the layer
that is of His Body, His members, directly and of Him indirectly.

In verses 9 through 15 we have the praising of the king in the
praising of the queen with the daughters of kings among the
king's most honorable women and the virgins, the queen's companions. (*Life-study of the Psalms*, pp. 260-261)

Today's Reading

The daughters of the kings [Psa. 45:9a] signify the believers of
Christ in their royalty, and the king's most prized (or, honorable,
glorious) women signify the believers of Christ in their honor and
majesty. Not only does the king have honor and majesty, but the
queen and the women around her also have honor and majesty.
This is a type, a picture, of the church with the believers.

Do you realize that…we all, males and females, are daughters
of kings because we have been born of the King and thus are of
the royal family.…If we are conscious of our royal status, our
behavior will be changed and our character will be uplifted. We
will not sell ourselves cheaply and we will not fight or quarrel
with others, but will behave ourselves more honorably.

From this Old Testament type we see that the believers are Christ's counterpart. In one sense, He is the King and we are the queen, His wife. In another sense, we are the components of the queen. These components are signified by the many virgins, the queen's companions. Since in verse 14 the words "virgins" and "companions" are in apposition, they refer to the same persons. According to the type, this signifies that the queen here is not an individual; rather, she is corporate, and all her companions are her components, with whom she is constituted and composed to be the wife of Christ the King.

Christ has only one queen, a corporate queen composed of the overcomers. The components of this queen are believers, but these believers are not the defeated ones. If they were defeated ones and not overcoming ones, they would not be honorable or majestic. I hope that we all will be among the overcomers and thus be components of the bride of Christ.

The queen [in verse 9] signifies the church, and her being covered with gold signifies the church's appearing in the divine nature....The daughter [in verse 10] is the queen, who signifies the church, and...this word about the daughter's forgetting her people and her father's house corresponds to the Lord's word about denying the natural relationships (Matt. 10:37; Luke 14:26) and caring for the church. Throughout the centuries, many believers have been persecuted by their family.

The queen's beauty [in Psalm 45:11] signifies the virtues of Christ expressed through the church,...[and] as the Lord of the church, Christ is worthy not only of her love but also of her worship.

Tyre...was a flourishing, commercial center known for its riches. [In verse 12] the daughter of Tyre signifies the people of the flourishing world....The rich have great wealth, but they do not have what this verse calls "favor."...The grace of God which we have in the church is the real favor....The rich will come to the church to obtain the grace of God. (*Life-study of the Psalms,* pp. 261-264)

Further Reading: Life-study of the Psalms, msg. 21

Enlightenment and inspiration: _____

_____

_____

_____

Morning Nourishment

Psa. **The king's daughter is all glorious within *the royal***
45:13-17 ***abode;* her garment is a woven work inwrought with**
gold. She will be led to the King in embroidered *cloth-*
***ing;* the virgins behind her, her companions, will be**
brought to You. They will be led with rejoicing and
exultation; they will enter the King's palace. In the
place of Your fathers will be Your sons; You will make
them princes in all the earth. I will cause Your name
to be remembered in all generations; therefore the
peoples will praise You forever and ever.

The king's daughter [Psa. 45:13a] is the queen signifying the church, and her being all glorious within the royal abode signifies the glorious church taking Christ as her royal abode.

First we, the believers of Christ, take Christ as our abode, and then we become His abode....The Lord Jesus said, "Abide in Me and I in you" (John 15:4a). This indicates that if we take Him as our abode, we become His abode.

This abode is a matter of experiencing Christ through the church. Christ, as the Son, is an abode to the Father and the Spirit, and His being such an abode involves the coinherence among the three of the Divine Trinity—the Father, the Son, and the Spirit. But when we believe in Christ, we enter into Him and take Him as our abode. Then, being in Him as our abode, we, the church, become His abode. (*Life-study of the Psalms*, pp. 264-265)

Today's Reading

[The] "woven work inwrought with gold" (Psa. 45:13b)...refers to the first layer of her covering—Christ as our righteousness through whom we are justified—signified by the gold of Ophir.

[The] embroidered clothing [v. 14a], another garment, the second layer of her covering, signifies that the church will be led to Christ at their marriage clothed with the righteousnesses of the saints to meet the requirement of Christ for their marriage.

Revelation 19:8 says, "It was given to her that she should be clothed in fine linen, bright and clean; for the fine linen is the righteousnesses of the saints." The word "righteousnesses" refers to Christ as our subjective righteousness, Christ lived out of us.... Thus, the queen in Psalm 45 has two garments. The first garment, the gold of Ophir, the woven work inwrought with gold, corresponds to Christ as our objective righteousness, which is for our salvation. The second garment, the embroidered clothing, corresponds to Christ as our subjective righteousnesses, which are for our victory.

Psalm 45:14b signifies that the overcoming saints will be invited to the marriage dinner of Christ (Rev. 19:9).

Psalm 45:15 signifies that the overcoming saints will enter, with rejoicing and exultation, the New Jerusalem as Christ's palace (Rev. 3:12).

In Psalm 45:16 and 17, we have the praising of the king in the praising of his sons, his descendants. Here, the sons of the king signify the members of Christ. On the one hand, as believers, we are the members of Christ; on the other hand, we are the sons, the descendants, of Christ.

In verse 16 "fathers" signifies Christ's forefathers in the flesh, and "sons" signifies the overcomers of Christ. The word "princes" signifies the overcomers of Christ reigning with Christ over the nations....When Christ reigns on earth, the overcomers will be His helpers in the kingship, His co-kings.

We need to see not only the beauty of Christ that is in Christ Himself and the beauty of Christ that is in the church but also the beauty of Christ that is in all His descendants, all His members, as the princes. If we see Christ's beauty in these three ways, we will have a complete view, the full picture, of His beauty.

Finally,...verse 17 reveals that Christ's name will be remembered in all generations through the overcoming saints and that Christ will be praised by the nations through His overcoming and co-reigning saints. (*Life-study of the Psalms,* pp. 265-268)

Further Reading: Life-study of the Psalms, msg. 21; *Christ and the Church Revealed and Typified in the Psalms,* ch. 7

Enlightenment and inspiration: _____

_____

_____

_____

Hymns, #1099

1   The queen in gold of Ophir
        At Thy right hand doth stand;
    King's daughters are the women
        Who fill Thy honored band.
    The church in all her glory
        Shall match her glorious King,
    And all the saints, the women,
        Thy likeness there shall bring.

2   O daughter, now consider,
        E'en now incline thine ear:
    Remember not thy people
        And all thine own things here.
    Thy beauty then shall blossom—
        'Twill be the King's desire;
    For He thy worthy Lord is,
        Thy worship to inspire.

3   The daughter's glorious garments
        Are made of inwrought gold—
    Within the inner palace,
        How wondrous to behold!
    The glory of God's nature
        Is given her to wear,
    That all His holy being
        She may in life declare.

4   In clothing too embroidered
        She'll to the King be led,
    In that fine linen garment
        To be exhibited.
    'Tis by the Spirit's stitching
        That Christ in us is wrought,
    And with this glorious garment
        We'll to the King be brought.

5   What gladness and rejoicing
        When we the King shall see!
    We'll shout His worthy praises
        Through all eternity.
    And though the King we worship
        Or glory in the Queen,
    In all this blest enjoyment
        The glory goes to Him.

Composition for prophecy with main point and sub-points: _____

Redemption through Christ's Ministry in the Stage of Incarnation

Scripture Reading: Rom. 3:24; Eph. 1:7; Gal. 3:13; 4:5; 1 John 1:7; 1 Pet. 1:18-19; Titus 2:14

Day 1   I. **To redeem is to purchase back at a cost (Rom. 3:24; 1 Cor. 6:20):**
   A. We were chosen and predestinated by God and originally belonged to God, but we became fallen and lost through sin; thus, we need redemption (Eph. 1:4-7).
   B. Man once was His possession, but man became fallen, sinking in sins and many things that were contrary to God's righteousness, holiness, and glory, thereby falling under the threefold demand of God's righteousness, holiness, and glory.
   C. Redemption deals with our sins by fulfilling God's requirements (Rom. 3:23-24; 8:4):
      1. The requirements of God's righteousness, holiness, and glory were so great upon us that it was impossible for us to fulfill them.
      2. Since we were unable to pay the price, God paid it for us through Christ's death on the cross, redeeming us at a tremendous cost (1 Pet. 1:18-19).
      3. Christ died on the cross to redeem us; His blood obtained eternal redemption for us (Gal. 3:13; Titus 2:14; Heb. 9:12; 1 Pet. 2:24; 3:18).

   II. **God has justified us by His grace through the redemption which is in Christ Jesus (Rom. 3:24):**
   A. Justification is God's action whereby He approves people according to His standard of righteousness; God does this on the basis of the redemption of Christ.
   B. Since Christ has paid the price for our sins and in His redemption has fulfilled all the

requirements on us, God, because He is just, must justify us freely (5:1; *Hymns,* #1003).

Day 2 **III. We have redemption in the Beloved through His blood (Eph. 1:6-7; Col. 1:13-14):**

A. The Beloved is God's beloved Son, the Son of His love, in whom He delights (Matt. 3:17; 17:5; Col. 1:13-14):

1. In the Beloved we were graced, made the object of God's favor and pleasure (Eph. 1:6).

2. As such an object, we enjoy God, and God enjoys us in His grace in His Beloved, who is His delight; in the Beloved we too become His delight.

B. In the Beloved "we have redemption through His blood, the forgiveness of offenses" (v. 7):

1. Christ's death accomplished redemption unto the forgiveness of our sins (Col. 1:14).

2. Redemption is what Christ accomplished for our offenses; forgiveness is the application of Christ's accomplishment to our offenses (Eph. 1:7).

3. The forgiveness of sins is the redemption that we have in Christ through His blood; apart from the shedding of blood, there is no forgiveness of sins (Heb. 9:22).

Day 3 **IV. The blood that has redeemed fallen human beings is the blood of Jesus, the Son of God (Acts 20:28; 1 John 1:7):**

A. As a man, the Lord Jesus had genuine human blood to shed for our redemption, and as God, He has the divine element that gives His blood eternal efficacy.

B. The Lord Jesus died on the cross as the God-man; the blood that He shed was not only the blood of the man Jesus but also the blood of the God-man:

1. In 1 John 1:7 the name *Jesus* denotes the Lord's humanity, which was needed for the shedding of the redeeming blood.

2. The title *His Son* denotes the Lord's divinity, which is needed for the eternal efficacy of the redeeming blood.

3. *The blood of Jesus His Son* indicates that this blood is the proper blood of a genuine man shed for the redeeming of God's fallen creatures, with the divine surety as its eternal efficacy; for this reason, the redemption accomplished by the God-man is eternal (Heb. 9:12).

Day 4

C. By His blood the Lord Jesus has released us from our sins and has purchased us for God (Rev. 1:5; 5:9).

V. **Christ has redeemed us out of the curse of the law (Gal. 3:13):**

A. In His work on the cross, Christ became a curse on our behalf and redeemed us out of the curse of the law:

1. When Christ took away our sin on the cross, He redeemed us out of the curse.

2. Not only did Christ redeem us out of the curse; He even became a curse on our behalf (v. 13; John 19:2, 5).

Day 5

B. Because Christ has redeemed us out of the curse of the law, having become a curse on our behalf, we may receive the greatest blessing, which is the Triune God—the Father, the Son, and the Spirit—as the processed, all-inclusive life-giving Spirit dwelling in us for our enjoyment (Gal. 3:14).

VI. **Christ has redeemed us from the custody of the law so that we might receive the sonship (4:4-5):**

A. Christ has redeemed us from the custody of the law so that we might receive the sonship and become the sons of God (3:23; 4:4-5).

B. Christ's redemption brings us into the sonship of God so that we may enjoy the divine life for the fulfillment of God's eternal purpose to have many sons for His corporate expression (vv. 4-5; Heb. 2:10; Rom. 8:29).

Day 6 **VII. The blood of Christ has redeemed us from our vain manner of life, a life that had no meaning and no goal (1 Pet. 1:18-19):**

A. In order to pass the time of our sojourning in fear, we need to have a deep realization concerning the redemption of Christ (v. 17).

B. Christ's redemption has separated us from our vain manner of life, and now we may be holy in all our manner of life (v. 15).

VIII. Christ gave Himself on our behalf not only to redeem us from all lawlessness but also to purify to Himself a people for His own possession—a people privately possessed by God as His unique, peculiar treasure, His own possession (Titus 2:14; Exo. 19:5; 1 Pet. 2:9).

Morning Nourishment

1 Pet. 1:19-20	...*The blood* of Christ; who was foreknown before the foundation of the world but has been manifested in the last of times for your sake.
Rom. 3:24	Being justified freely by His grace through the redemption which is in Christ Jesus.
1 Cor. 6:20	For you have been bought with a price. So then glorify God in your body.

God created...man as the head and center [of the universe]. Then man fell. In the eyes of God, man's fall involved the entire creation. To redeem this fallen creation God came in the Son.

Redemption was not an afterthought. It was preordained by God. First Peter 1:19-20 tells us that the Redeemer, Christ, was foreknown by God before the foundation of the world. In this verse "world" refers to the entire universe. Before the foundation of the universe, God knew that man would fall. Thus, God preordained the Son, Christ, to be the Redeemer. We can see from this that God's redemption was not accidental.

Furthermore, Revelation 13:8 says that the Lamb...was slain "from the foundation of the world."...In God's view [Christ] was slain from the day creation came into existence because God foreknew that His creation would fall.

These verses show that God's redemption was not an afterthought, but rather something ordained, planned, and prepared by God in eternity past. How we should treasure this fact about the redemption we enjoy in Christ! (*The Basic Revelation in the Holy Scriptures*, pp. 19-20)

Today's Reading

Romans 3:22-24 reveals...that the believers are justified by God and receive the righteousness of God through the redemption of Christ.

The word *redeem* means to purchase back something that originally was ours but that had become lost. In other words, redemption means to repossess at a cost. We originally belonged to God; we were His possession. However, we were lost. Nevertheless, God did not give us up. He paid the price to have us back....Because we were lost, we had many problems with God....We were under a threefold demand, the demand of righteousness, holiness, and glory. Many requirements were laid upon us, and it was impossible for us to fulfill them. The price was too great. God paid the price for us, repossessing us at a tremendous cost. Christ died on the cross to accomplish eternal redemption for us (Gal. 3:13; 1 Pet. 2:24; 3:18; 2 Cor. 5:21; Heb. 10:12; 9:28). His blood has obtained eternal redemption for us (vv. 12, 14; 1 Pet. 1:18-19). (*The Conclusion of the New Testament,* pp. 3023, 3037-3038)

Justification is God's action in approving people according to His standard of righteousness,...not ours....Regardless of how righteous we are or how righteous we think we are, our righteousness is just a fraction of an inch high. How high is God's righteousness? It is unlimited! Can you be approved by God according to your own righteousness? This is impossible. Although you may be right with everyone—with your parents, your children, and your friends—your righteousness will never justify you before God. You may justify yourself according to your standard of righteousness, but that does not enable you to be justified by God according to His standard. We need justification by faith. Justification by faith before God means we are approved by God according to the standard of His righteousness.

[God] can do [this] because our justification is based upon the redemption of Christ. When the redemption of Christ is applied to us, we are justified. If there were no such redemption, it would be impossible for us to be justified by God. Redemption is the basis of justification. (*Life-study of Romans,* p. 51)

Since Christ has paid the price for our sins and in His redemption has fulfilled all of God's requirements on us, God, because He is just, must justify us freely. (*The Conclusion of the New Testament,* p. 3024)

Further Reading: The Basic Revelation in the Holy Scriptures, ch. 2; *The Conclusion of the New Testament,* msgs. 296-297

Enlightenment and inspiration: _____

Morning Nourishment

Eph. To the praise of the glory of His grace, with which He
1:6-7 graced us in the Beloved; in whom we have redemption through His blood, the forgiveness of offenses,
according to the riches of His grace.

Col. Who delivered us out of the authority of darkness and
1:13-14 transferred *us* into the kingdom of the Son of His love,
in whom we have redemption, the forgiveness of sins.

Ephesians 1:6 says that God has graced us in the Beloved.
Here Paul does not say "in Christ" or "in Him"; he says "in the
Beloved." The Beloved is God's beloved Son in whom He delights
(Matt. 3:17; 17:5)....For God to grace us is to make us an object
in whom He delights. This is altogether a pleasure to God. In
Christ we have been blessed by God with every blessing. In the
Beloved we were graced, made the object of God's favor and plea-
sure. As such an object we enjoy God, and God enjoys us in His
grace in His Beloved, who is His delight. In His Beloved we also
become His delight. (*Life-study of Ephesians*, p. 52)

Today's Reading

God delights in the Beloved, and He delights also in us. The
phrase "in the Beloved" conveys the full delight, satisfaction, and
enjoyment God the Father has in us because we have been made
the object of His grace and delight. In this sense we should all
appreciate ourselves and ever esteem ourselves highly because we
are the object of God's delight....We should have such a view about
ourselves, not according to our natural state, but according to the
fact that we have been chosen, predestinated, regenerated, and
graced. God delights in us, not in ourselves but in His Beloved.

Although God delights in us and has made us the objects of
His grace, we still need redemption because...our Father who
delights in us is righteous and cannot tolerate unrighteousness,
wrongdoings, or offenses. Such things insult His righteousness.
Therefore, His righteousness makes the accomplishment of
redemption necessary. Redemption fulfills God's righteous
requirements and pleases God. God is not only a God of love; He is

also righteous, and anything unrighteous displeases Him. Everything related to Him must satisfy the requirements of His righteousness. This is the reason that, in order to please God, the beloved Son had to go to the cross to accomplish full redemption for God's chosen ones.

The Son's redemption is through His blood shed on the cross for our sins (1 Pet. 1:18-19). Because the Son's death in the flesh on the cross has fulfilled God's righteous requirement, His blood becomes the very instrument for our redemption.

The Son's redemption through His blood is the forgiveness of our offenses (Matt. 26:28; Heb. 9:22). Redemption is what Christ has accomplished for our offenses; forgiveness is what Christ accomplished applied to our offenses. Redemption was accomplished on the cross, whereas forgiveness is applied the moment we believe in Christ. Redemption and forgiveness are actually two ends of one thing....Although redemption was accomplished on the cross when Christ shed His blood, it was not applied to us at that time. The application did not take place until we believed in Christ and made confession to the righteous God. At that very moment, the Spirit of God applied to us the redemption Christ had accomplished on the cross. Hence, redemption is the accomplishment, and forgiveness is the application.

The Bible says that without the shedding of blood there is no forgiveness of sins. Therefore, in order for us to be forgiven, blood had to be shed....For the actual accomplishment of redemption, there had to be the blood of a higher life, a blood altogether sinless. ...Moreover, God's chosen ones number in the millions....Therefore, in addition to a perfect, sinless blood, there was the need of a sin offering that could include millions....Only Jesus Christ could be the sin offering with a sinless blood shed for these millions of chosen ones. By the shedding of His blood once upon the cross, the eternal redemption of God's chosen ones was accomplished once for all (Heb. 9:28; 10:10, 12). (*Life-study of Ephesians,* pp. 52-53, 57-59)

Further Reading: Life-study of Ephesians, msgs. 5-6

Enlightenment and inspiration: _____
_____
_____
_____

Morning Nourishment

Acts Take heed to yourselves and to all the flock, among
20:28 whom the Holy Spirit has placed you as overseers
to shepherd the church of God, which He obtained
through His own blood.

1 John But if we walk in the light as He is in the light, we
1:7 have fellowship with one another, and the blood of
Jesus His Son cleanses us from every sin.

Heb. And not through the blood of goats and calves but
9:12 through His own blood, entered once for all into the
Holy of Holies, obtaining an eternal redemption.

According to Matthew 1 and Luke 1, the Lord Jesus was conceived of the Holy Spirit. Later, for His ministry, He was anointed with the Holy Spirit, who descended upon Him (Luke 3:22).

When the Lord Jesus was on the cross dying for our sins, God was in Him essentially. Therefore, the One who died for our sins was the God-man. But at a certain point the righteous God, while judging this God-man, left Him economically. God's forsaking of Christ was an economical matter related to the carrying out of God's judgment.

Because the Lord Jesus was conceived of the Holy Spirit and was born of God and with God, He had the Holy Spirit as the intrinsic essence of His divine being. Therefore, it was not possible for God to leave, to forsake, Him essentially. Nevertheless, He was forsaken by God economically when the Spirit, who had descended upon Him as the economical power for the carrying out of His ministry, left Him. But the essence of God remained in His being. Therefore, He died on the cross as the God-man, and the blood He shed there for our redemption was…the blood of the God-man. Therefore, this blood, through which God obtained the church, is God's own blood [Acts 20:28]. (*Life-study of Acts,* pp. 472-473)

Today's Reading

The conception and birth of the Lord Jesus was God's incarnation (John 1:14), constituted of the divine essence added to the human essence, hence, producing the God-man of two natures—

divinity and humanity. Through this, God joined Himself to humanity that He might be manifested in the flesh (1 Tim. 3:16) and might
be the Savior (Luke 2:11) who died and shed His blood for us.

The blood that has redeemed fallen human beings is the blood
of Jesus, the Son of God. As human beings, we need genuine
human blood for our redemption. Because He was a man, the Lord
Jesus could fulfill this requirement. As a man, He shed human
blood to redeem fallen human beings. The Lord is also the Son of
God, even God Himself. Therefore, with His blood there is the element of eternity, and this element ensures the eternal efficacy of
His blood. Therefore, as a man He had genuine human blood, and
as God He has the element that gives to His blood eternal efficacy.

First John 1:7 says that "the blood of Jesus His Son cleanses us
from every sin."…"The blood of Jesus His Son" indicates that this
blood is the proper blood of a genuine man for redeeming God's
fallen creatures with the divine surety for its eternal efficacy, an
efficacy which is all-prevailing in space and everlasting in time.…
The redemption accomplished by the God-man, by the One mingled with God, is eternal.

If the redemption accomplished on the cross was accomplished
merely by a man, that redemption could not be eternally effective…
[and] would not be effective for the redemption of millions of believers.…Although man is limited, God is not limited.…Although
man is temporal, God is eternal. Therefore, in Christ's redemption
there is the eternal and unlimited element of God.…[Thus],…this
redemption is called an eternal redemption [Heb. 9:12].

We need to see that the blood shed by the Lord Jesus on the
cross is eternal blood. It is the blood not merely of a man but of a
man mingled with the divine element. Hence, this blood, the
blood of Jesus, the Son of God, is eternal. In Acts 20:28 Paul had
the boldness to speak of this blood as being God's own blood. (*Life-
study of Acts,* pp. 469-470)

Further Reading: Life-study of Acts, msg. 54; *God's New Testament
Economy,* ch. 3

Enlightenment and inspiration: _____
_____
_____
_____

Morning Nourishment

Rev. And from Jesus Christ, the faithful Witness, the First-
1:5 born of the dead, and the Ruler of the kings of the
earth. To Him who loves us and has released us from
our sins by His blood.

5:9 And they sing a new song, saying: You are worthy to
take the scroll and to open its seals, for You were slain
and have purchased for God by Your blood *men* out of
every tribe and tongue and people and nation.

Gal. Christ has redeemed us out of the curse of the law,
3:13 having become a curse on our behalf; because it is
written, "Cursed is everyone hanging on a tree."

Revelation 1:5...indicates that, as priests of God, we have been
released from our sins by the blood of Christ.

The word "released" in 1:5 implies a fight or a struggle. This fight
was caused by the fact that Satan was using our sins to hold us. But
in this matter Satan has been defeated by the redeeming blood of
Christ, the blood that...released us from the hold of our sins.

The redemption through Christ's blood has made us priests to
Him (1 Pet. 2:5), those who express God's image. This is the kingly,
royal priesthood (1 Pet. 2:9) for the fulfillment of God's original
purpose in creating man (Gen. 1:26-28). This kingly priesthood is
being exercised in today's church life (Rev. 5:10). It will be inten-
sively practiced in the millennial kingdom (Rev. 20:6), and it will
be ultimately consummated in the New Jerusalem (Rev. 22:3, 5).
(*The Conclusion of the New Testament,* p. 1098)

Today's Reading

In Revelation 5:9 we see that, in order to make us priests
(v. 10), the Lord Jesus purchased us to God by His blood. On the
negative side, the blood of Christ has released us from the usur-
pation of Satan; on the positive side, His blood has purchased us
back to God to be His possession. As those purchased to God by
the blood of Christ, we are now priests of God.

In His work on the cross Christ became a curse on our behalf
and redeemed us out of the curse of the law...(Gal. 3:13). Christ as

our Substitute on the cross not only bore the curse for us but also became a curse for us. The curse of the law issued from the sin of man (Gen. 3:17). When Christ took away our sin on the cross, He redeemed us out of the curse. Because the problem of sin has been solved, the problem of the curse has been solved as well.

As descendants of Adam, all sinners are under the curse. In Romans 5 we see that Adam brought us all under the curse. However, the curse was not made official until the law was given. Now the law declares that all the fallen descendants of Adam are under the curse. Whereas the law condemns us and makes the curse official, Christ through His crucifixion has redeemed us out of the curse of the law. On the cross He was even made a curse for us. Therefore, the curse that came in through Adam's fall has been dealt with by Christ's redemption.

The origin of the curse is man's sin. God brought in the curse after Adam's sin, saying, "Cursed is the ground because of you" (Gen. 3:17). The sign of the curse is thorns. For this reason, after Adam's sin, the earth brought forth thorns. Furthermore,…the curse is related to the law of God; it is the demand of the righteous God upon sinners.

When Christ bore our sins, He also took our curse. The crown of thorns indicates this (John 19:2, 5). Since thorns are a sign of the curse, Christ's wearing a crown of thorns indicates that He took our curse on the cross. Because Christ was cursed in our place, the demand of the law was fulfilled, and He could redeem us from the curse of the law.

Not only did Christ redeem us out from the curse; He even became a curse on our behalf. This indicates that He was absolutely abandoned by God. God forsook Christ economically and also considered Him a curse. On the cross Christ accomplished the great work…to bear our sins and to remove the curse. (*The Conclusion of the New Testament,* pp. 1098, 766-767)

Further Reading: The Conclusion of the New Testament, msgs. 70-71;
    Life-study of Galatians, msg. 12

Enlightenment and inspiration: _____

_____
_____
_____

Morning Nourishment

**Gal. In order that the blessing of Abraham might come to
3:14 the Gentiles in Christ Jesus, that we might receive
the promise of the Spirit through faith.
4:4-5 But when the fullness of the time came, God sent
forth His Son, born of a woman, born under law, that
He might redeem those under law that we might
receive the sonship.**

["The blessing" in Galatians 3:14 is] the blessing promised by
God to Abraham (Gen. 12:3) for all the nations of the earth. The
promise was fulfilled, and the blessing has come to the nations in
Christ through His redemption by the cross. (Gal. 3:14, footnote 1)

In the gospel we have received not only the blessing of forgiveness, washing, and cleansing; even more, we have received the
greatest blessing, which is the Triune God—the Father, Son, and
Spirit—as the processed, all-inclusive life-giving Spirit dwelling
in us in a most subjective way for our enjoyment. Oh, what a
blessing that we can enjoy such an all-inclusive One as our daily
portion! (footnote 2)

Today's Reading

The Spirit as revealed in Paul's writings is the Father, the Son,
and the Spirit processed to become the all-inclusive life-giving
Spirit. This Spirit enters into the believers to be their life and
everything to them. Such a Spirit is the total blessing of the gospel
…[and] includes forgiveness, redemption, salvation, reconcilia-
tion, justification, eternal life, the divine nature, the uplifted and
resurrected human nature, and the very Triune God Himself.

"The fullness of the time" in Galatians 4:4 denotes the completion of the Old Testament time, which occurred at the time
appointed of the Father (v. 2). In verse 4 Paul describes the Son as
"born of a woman, born under law." The woman is, of course, the
virgin Mary (Luke 1:27-35). The Son of God came of her to be the
seed of the woman, as promised in Genesis 3:15. Furthermore,
Christ was born under law, as revealed in Luke 2:21-24, 27, and
He kept the law, as the four Gospels reveal.

God's chosen people were shut up by law under its custody (Gal. 3:23). Christ was born under law in order to redeem them from its custody that they might receive the sonship and become the sons of God. Hence, they should not return to the custody of law to be under its slavery as the Galatians had been seduced to do, but should remain in the sonship of God to enjoy the life supply of the Spirit in Christ. According to the entire revelation of the New Testament, God's economy is to produce sons. Sonship is the focal point of God's economy....God's economy is the dispensing of Himself into His chosen people to make them His sons. Christ's redemption is to bring us into the sonship of God that we may enjoy the divine life. It is not God's economy to make us keepers of law, obeying the commandments and ordinances of the law, which was given only for a temporary purpose. God's economy is to make us sons of God, inheriting the blessing of God's promise, which was given for His eternal purpose. His eternal purpose is to have many sons for His corporate expression (Heb. 2:10; Rom. 8:29). Hence, He predestinated us unto sonship (Eph. 1:5) and regenerated us to be His sons (John 1:12-13). We should remain in His sonship that we may become His heirs to inherit all He has planned for His eternal expression and should not be distracted to Judaism by the appreciation of law.

Since we have the Spirit of sonship, we no longer need to be held under the custody of the law. We do not need the law to be our guardian, steward, or child-conductor. In Galatians 4:7 Paul says, "So then you are no longer a slave but a son; and if a son, an heir also through God." The New Testament believer is no longer a slave to works under law but a son in life under grace. Instead of the law to keep us in custody, we have the all-inclusive Spirit. This Spirit is everything to us. Whereas the law could not give life, the Spirit gives life and brings us into maturity that we may have the full position and right of sons. The custody of the law has been replaced by the Spirit of sonship. (*Life-study of Galatians,* pp. 130, 190-191, 197)

Further Reading: Life-study of Galatians, msgs. 15, 22

Enlightenment and inspiration: _____

_____

_____

_____

Morning Nourishment

1 Pet. **Knowing that *it was* not with corruptible things,**
1:18-19 **with silver or gold, *that* you were redeemed from**
your vain manner of life handed down from your
fathers, but with precious blood, as of a Lamb with-
out blemish and without spot, *the blood* of Christ.
Titus **Who gave Himself for us that He might redeem us**
2:14 **from all lawlessness and purify to Himself a particu-**
lar people as His unique possession, zealous of good
works.

First Peter 1:18 says, "Knowing that it was not with corruptible things, with silver or gold, that you were redeemed from your
vain manner of life handed down from your fathers." According to
grammar, verse 18 is related to "pass the time of your sojourning
in fear" in verse 17. This indicates that in order to pass the time of
our sojourning in fear, we need a deep realization concerning the
redemption of Christ. Today many Christians are living in a loose
way because their understanding of Christ's redemption is shallow. (*Life-study of 1 Peter,* p. 97)

Today's Reading

When I was a child studying in the elementary school of a
Baptist mission, I heard much about the cross of Christ and
Christ's redemption. However, nothing that I heard touched my
heart, for that teaching regarding the redemption of Christ was
shallow. I do not know why the missionaries and the Chinese min-
isters did not say something weighty from 1 Peter 1:18
and 19....Peter's way of speaking about redemption in these
verses is far from superficial.

According to verse 18, the blood of Christ has redeemed us from
our vain manner of life. This vain manner of life is in contrast to the
holy manner of life in verse 15. According to most other references
in Scripture, the blood of Christ redeems us from sins, transgres-
sions, lawlessness, and all sinful things (Eph. 1:7; Heb. 9:15; Titus
2:14). Here is an exception: Christ's blood has redeemed us from
our old, vain manner of life, because the emphasis here is not on

sinfulness but on the manner of life. The whole chapter emphasizes the holy manner of life which God's chosen people should have in their sojourn. Not only is the Spirit's sanctification for this; even Christ's redemption is for this—to separate us from our vain manner of life handed down from our fathers. Knowing that this was accomplished with the highest price, the precious blood of Christ, we pass the days of our sojourning in fear.

Our old manner of life, a life in lusts (1 Pet. 1:14), had no meaning and no goal; hence, it was vain. But now to live a holy life, to express God in His holiness, is our goal (vv. 15-16).

Many precious biblical terms...have become common and religious;...they have been spoiled. The word "redeemed" is an example....When we read this word in the Bible, we may not have much feeling within us concerning it. However, when Peter wrote 1:18 and 19, he was full of feeling.

Christ died on the cross and shed His precious blood to redeem us. From our side, we were purchased, but from Satan's side, we were redeemed....Only the blood of Christ was qualified and sufficient to redeem us, to purchase us. We had been put on sale by the enemy Satan, our usurper. But Christ, our Redeemer, paid the highest price to purchase us. (*Life-study of 1 Peter,* pp. 97-99)

In Titus 2:14 Paul says that Christ "gave Himself for us that He might redeem us from all lawlessness and purify to Himself a particular people as His unique possession, zealous of good works." The words "for us" here mean on our behalf. They do not mean instead of us. To redeem means to buy with a price (1 Cor. 6:20; 1 Pet. 1:18-19; 1 Tim. 2:6). Christ gave Himself for us not only that He might redeem us from all lawlessness but also purify to Himself a people for His own possession. A people for His possession are a peculiar people. This expression is borrowed from the Old Testament (Deut. 7:6; 14:2; 26:18) and denotes a people privately possessed by God as His peculiar treasure (Exo. 19:5), His own possession (1 Pet. 2:9). (*Life-study of Titus,* pp. 35-36)

Further Reading: Life-study of 1 Peter, msgs. 12, 18

Enlightenment and inspiration: _____
_____

_____

_____

Hymns, #1003

1   Why should I worry, doubt and fear?
Has God not caused His Son to bear
   My sins upon the tree?
The debt that Christ for me has paid,
Would God another mind have made
   To claim again from me?

2   Redemption full the Lord has made,
And all my debts has fully paid,
   From law to set me free.
I fear not for the wrath of God,
For I've been sprinkled with His blood,
   It wholly covers me.

3   For me forgiveness He has gained,
And full acquittal was obtained,
   All debts of sin are paid;
God would not have His claim on two,
First on His Son, my Surety true,
   And then upon me laid.

4   So now I have full peace and rest,
My Savior Christ hath done the best
   And set me wholly free;
By His all-efficacious blood
I ne'er could be condemned by God,
   For He has died for me!

Composition for prophecy with main point and sub-points: _____

_____

_____

_____

_____

_____

_____

_____

_____

_____

_____

_____

_____

_____

_____

_____

_____

_____

_____

_____

_____

_____

_____

_____

_____

_____

_____

_____

_____

_____

_____

_____

_____

_____

_____

_____

_____

_____

_____

_____

_____

Experiencing, Enjoying, and Ministering Christ in the Stage of Inclusion

Scripture Reading: Exo. 30:22-25; Acts 13:33; 1 Cor. 15:45b; 1 Pet. 1:3; Rom. 5:10; Psa. 23

Day 1   **I. The second stage of Christ's full ministry is the stage of inclusion, from His resurrection to the degradation of the church:**

A. The stage of incarnation was the stage of Christ's first "becoming"—the stage of His becoming flesh (John 1:14).

B. The stage of inclusion is the stage of Christ's second "becoming"—the stage of His becoming the life-giving Spirit (1 Cor. 15:45b).

C. Our use of the word *inclusion* is based on our use of the word *inclusive;* for Christ, as the last Adam, to become the life-giving Spirit was for Him to become the all-inclusive Spirit (Phil. 1:19; Exo. 30:22-25; cf. Gen. 17:1).

Day 2   **II. Christ's ministry in the stage of inclusion is His ministry in resurrection as the life-giving Spirit in our spirit; resurrection is the life pulse and lifeline of the divine economy (1 Cor. 15:12-19, 31-36, 45-49, 54-58):**

A. If there were no resurrection, God would be the God of the dead, not of the living (Matt. 22:32).

B. If there were no resurrection, Christ would not have been raised from the dead; He would be a dead Savior, not a living One who lives forever (Rev. 1:18) and is able to save to the uttermost (Heb. 7:25; Rom. 5:10).

C. If there were no resurrection, there would be no living proof of our being justified by His death (4:25), no imparting of life (John 12:24), no regeneration (3:5), no renewing (Titus 3:5), no transformation (Rom. 12:2; 2 Cor. 3:18), and no conformity to the image of Christ (Rom. 8:29).

D. If there were no resurrection, there would be no

members of Christ (12:5), no Body of Christ
as His fullness (Eph. 1:20-23), no church as
Christ's bride (John 3:29), and therefore no new
man (Eph. 2:15; 4:24; Col. 3:10-11).

E. If there were no resurrection, God's New Testament economy would altogether collapse, and
God's eternal purpose would be nullified (Acts
13:33; 1 Pet. 1:3; 1 Cor. 15:45b; Col. 1:18).

Day 3 **III. We need to see and enter into the unveiled
truth of Christ's resurrection in the stage
of inclusion for the ultimate goal of God's
economy:**

A. In resurrection Christ was born to be the firstborn Son of God (Acts 13:33):

1. From eternity past without beginning,
Christ was God's only begotten Son, possessing only divinity, without humanity
and not having passed through death into
resurrection (John 1:18).

2. In incarnation the only begotten Son of God
became flesh to be a God-man, a man possessing both the divine nature and the
human nature.

3. Through death and resurrection Christ in
the flesh as the seed of David was designated to be the firstborn Son of God (Rom.
1:3-4):

a. In death His humanity was crucified
(1 Pet. 3:18).

b. In resurrection His crucified humanity
was made alive by the Spirit of His divinity and was uplifted into the sonship of
the only begotten Son of God; thus,
He was begotten by God in His resurrection to be the firstborn Son of God (Rom.
8:29).

Day 4   B. In resurrection Christ became the life-giving
Spirit (1 Cor. 15:45b):

1. The life-giving Spirit "was not yet" before

the resurrection of Christ—the glorification of Christ (John 7:39).

2. Christ, the Son of God as the second of the
Divine Trinity, after completing His ministry on the earth, became (was transfigured
into) the life-giving Spirit in His resurrection to release the divine life that was confined in the shell of His humanity and to
dispense it into His believers, making them
the many members which constitute His
Body (12:24; cf. 19:34).

3. This life-giving Spirit, who is the pneumatic Christ, is also called:

a. The Spirit of life (Rom. 8:2).

b. The Spirit of Jesus (Acts 16:7).

c. The Spirit of Christ (Rom. 8:9).

d. The Spirit of Jesus Christ (Phil. 1:19).

e. The Lord Spirit (2 Cor. 3:18).

Day 5　C. In resurrection we, God's chosen ones, were
regenerated (1 Pet. 1:3):

1. The pneumatic Christ became the firstborn
Son of God and the life-giving Spirit for the
regenerating of the believers, making them
the many sons of God born of God with Him
in one great universal delivery.

2. This great birth of the firstborn Son of God
and of the many sons of God in Christ's resurrection was for the composition of the
house of God and for the constitution of
the Body of Christ to be His fullness, His
expression and expansion, to consummate
the eternal expression and expansion of the
processed and consummated Triune God
(Eph. 1:23; 3:19; Rev. 21:10-11).

3. In the one Spirit all the believers of Christ
have been baptized into the one Body of
Christ and have been given to drink this
Spirit (1 Cor. 12:13).

4. The Christ in resurrection gives Himself as

the all-inclusive life-giving Spirit without measure through His speaking of the words of God (John 3:34).

5. All the believers in Christ are built up into a dwelling place of God in their spirit indwelt by Him as the Spirit (Eph. 2:22) through the process of His organic salvation (Rom. 5:10)—through dispositional sanctification (15:16), renewing (Titus 3:5), transformation (2 Cor. 3:18), and conformation (Rom. 8:29) unto glorification (Phil. 3:21).

Day 6 **IV. We need to establish and shepherd the churches by the pneumatic Christ, the Christ who is the life-giving Spirit, with His organic salvation:**

A. The Lord Jesus has incorporated the apostolic ministry with His heavenly ministry to take care of God's flock, which is the church, issuing in the Body of Christ (John 21:15-17; Acts 20:28; 1 Pet. 5:2; 1 Cor. 15:58; cf. Gen. 48:15-16a).

B. The shepherding of the pneumatic Christ is in five stages (Psa. 23):

1. The enjoyment of Christ as the green pastures and of the Spirit as the waters of rest (v. 2).

2. The revival and transformation on the paths of righteousness (v. 3).

3. The experience of the resurrected pneumatic Christ while walking through the valley of the shadow of death (v. 4).

4. The deeper and higher enjoyment of the resurrected Christ in fighting against the adversaries (v. 5).

5. The lifelong enjoyment of the divine goodness and lovingkindness in the house of Jehovah as the ultimate goal of God's eternal economy (v. 6).

Morning Nourishment

Exo.   **You also take the finest spices: of flowing myrrh**
30:23-25 **five hundred *shekels*, and of fragrant cinnamon**
          half as much, two hundred fifty *shekels*, and of fra-
          grant calamus two hundred fifty *shekels*, and of
          cassia five hundred *shekels*, according to the
          shekel of the sanctuary, and a hin of olive oil. And
          you shall make it a holy anointing oil, a fragrant
          ointment compounded according to the work of a
          compounder; it shall be a holy anointing oil.

1 Cor.   **...The last Adam *became* a life-giving Spirit.**
15:45

In His resurrection the Christ who had become flesh through
incarnation became the life-giving Spirit (1 Cor. 15:45b). Christ,
therefore, has had two becomings. The first becoming is seen in
John 1:14—the Word became flesh. The second becoming is seen
in 1 Corinthians 15:45b—the last Adam (Christ in the flesh) became
the life-giving Spirit....Christ's becoming the life-giving Spirit in
resurrection involves something that we may designate by the
word *inclusion*.

Christ's becoming flesh through incarnation was rather simple, for it involved just two parties—the Holy Spirit and a human
virgin (Luke 1:26-27, 30-32, 35). Christ's becoming the life-giving
Spirit, on the contrary, was not simple, for it involved and included
divinity, humanity, Christ's death with its effectiveness, and
Christ's resurrection with its power. In and through Christ's resurrection six things were compounded together to become the life-
giving Spirit, which is God's anointing ointment (1 John 2:20, 27).

The compound life-giving Spirit is typified by the anointing ointment in Exodus 30:23-25. Without these verses in Exodus 30, it
would be difficult for us to understand how the life-giving Spirit has
been compounded with God, man, Christ's death, Christ's resurrection, the effectiveness of Christ's death, and the power of Christ's
resurrection. (*Incarnation, Inclusion, and Intensification*, pp. 7-8)

Today's Reading

The anointing ointment in Exodus was a compound of one

main item—a hin of olive oil—compounded with four kinds of spices: myrrh, cinnamon, calamus, and cassia....The one hin of olive oil signifies God. The number one signifies God, and the number four (four spices) signifies man as God's creature. In particular, here the number four signifies the incarnated Christ as a human being. Myrrh signifies Christ's death, and cinnamon signifies the sweet effectiveness of Christ's death. Calamus is a reed that grows in a marsh or muddy place, shooting upward toward the sky; thus calamus signifies Christ's resurrection. Cassia is a kind of bark used as a repellent to repel snakes and insects. Therefore, cassia signifies the power, especially the repelling power, of Christ's resurrection.

What we have in Exodus 30 is the compound ointment as a type of the compound life-giving Spirit. The actual compounding of the Spirit took place in Christ's resurrection. It was in resurrection that the very God embodied in Christ and mingled with His humanity was compounded with Christ's death, the effectiveness of Christ's death, Christ's resurrection, and the power of His resurrection to produce the compound Spirit. This compounding was a matter of inclusion, for in the compound life-giving Spirit six items are included. Hence, the life-giving Spirit may be called the all-inclusive Spirit, the Spirit who includes divinity, humanity, the death of Christ and its effectiveness, and the resurrection of Christ and its power.

Whereas the incarnation was an objective matter, this inclusion is subjective to us and applicable to us in our experience. According to John 20:22 in the evening of the day of His resurrection, the Lord Jesus came as the compound Spirit and breathed into the disciples, saying, "Receive the Holy Spirit."...As a part of the Body, those disciples represented the Body in receiving the inclusion, in receiving the compound Spirit. Because we can experience Christ in the stage of inclusion in such a subjective way, in this stage He is more applicable to us than He was in the stage of incarnation. (*Incarnation, Inclusion, and Intensification,* pp. 9-10)

Further Reading: Incarnation, Inclusion, and Intensification, ch. 1

Enlightenment and inspiration: _____
_____
_____

Morning Nourishment

1 Cor.   But if Christ is proclaimed that He has been raised
15:12-17 from the dead, how *is it that* some among you say that
         there is no resurrection of the dead? But if there is no
         resurrection of the dead, neither has Christ been
         raised. And if Christ has not been raised, then our
         proclamation is vain; your faith is vain also. And also
         we are found to be false witnesses of God because we
         have testified concerning God that He raised Christ,
         whom He did not raise, if indeed the dead are not
         raised. For if the dead are not raised, neither has
         Christ been raised. And if Christ has not been raised,
         your faith is futile; you are still in your sins.

   58   Therefore, my beloved brothers, be steadfast, immov-
         able, always abounding in the work of the Lord,
         knowing that your labor is not in vain in the Lord.

Because so many complications are involved in Christ's
second becoming, His becoming the all-inclusive life-giving
Spirit in resurrection, we may use the word *inclusion* in
speaking of this second stage of Christ. The issue of this
becoming was not something simple but something compounded, that is, not just oil signifying the Spirit of God but
the ointment signifying the life-giving Spirit, the Spirit who
gives life. This Spirit is the pneumatic Christ, the Christ in
the second stage—the stage of inclusion. (*Incarnation, Inclusion, and Intensification,* p. 17)

Today's Reading

Christ's resurrection...produced the firstborn Son of God
by uplifting the humanity of Christ into His divinity and by
having Christ born of God (Acts 13:33; Psa. 2:7), that is, by
designating the seed of David (Christ's human nature) by the
Spirit of holiness (the divinity of Christ) in the power of resurrection to be the firstborn Son of God (Rom. 1:3-4). In Christ's
resurrection all of God's chosen people were regenerated to be
the many sons of God and the many brothers of the firstborn

Son of God (1 Pet. 1:3; Heb. 2:10; Rom. 8:29). In Christ's resurrection the Spirit of God was consummated to be the life-giving Spirit (1 Cor. 15:45b): the Spirit of Christ—the pneumatic Christ, the pneumatized Christ (Rom. 8:9); the ultimate consummation of the processed and consummated Triune God, who is embodied in the pneumatized Christ as the life-giving Spirit; and the reality of resurrection, which is Christ Himself and the processed and consummated Triune God (John 11:25; 1 John 5:6). From this we can see that Christ's resurrection is full of complications. (*Incarnation, Inclusion, and Intensification,* p. 17)

In 1 Corinthians 15 the apostle deals with the Corinthians' heretical saying that there is no resurrection of the dead.... This is the tenth problem among them. It is the most damaging and destructive to God's New Testament economy....Resurrection is the life pulse and lifeline of the divine economy. If there were no resurrection, God would be the God of the dead, not the God of the living (Matt. 22:32). If there were no resurrection, Christ would not have been raised from the dead. He would be a dead Savior, not the One who lives forever (Rev. 1:18) and is able to save to the uttermost (Heb. 7:25). If there were no resurrection, there would be no living proof of justification by His death (Rom. 4:25), no imparting of life (John 12:24), no regeneration (John 3:5), no renewing (Titus 3:5), no transformation (Rom. 12:2; 2 Cor. 3:18), and no conformity to the image of Christ (Rom. 8:29). If there were no resurrection, there would be no members of Christ (Rom. 12:5), no Body of Christ as His fullness (Eph. 1:20-23), and no church as Christ's bride (John 3:29) and the new man (Eph. 2:15; 4:24; Col. 3:10-11). If there were no resurrection, God's New Testament economy would altogether collapse and God's eternal purpose would be nullified. (*Life Study of 1 Corinthians,* pp. 593-594)

Further Reading: Incarnation, Inclusion, and Intensification, ch. 2

Enlightenment and inspiration: _____

_____

_____

_____

Morning Nourishment

Acts **That God has fully fulfilled this *promise* to us their**
13:33 **children in raising up Jesus, as it is also written in**
the second Psalm, "You are My Son; this day have I
begotten You."

From eternity past without beginning, Christ was God's only
begotten Son. As such, He possessed only divinity and was without humanity, because He had not yet become flesh to pass
through death and enter into resurrection. In the Gospel of John
the Lord said, "I am the resurrection and the life" (11:25)....To be
resurrected is to overcome and transcend death, that is, to enter
into and come out of death. As the only begotten Son of God,
Christ is resurrection from eternity, but then He did not have the
experience of resurrection. It was not until after He had accomplished His ministry in the flesh through His death that He
entered into resurrection. (*How to Be a Co-worker and an Elder*
and How to Fulfill Their Obligations, pp. 27-28)

Today's Reading

In His incarnation the only begotten Son of God became flesh
to be a God-man, a man possessing both the divine nature and the
human nature.

Romans 1:3-4 tells us that through His death and resurrection
Christ in the flesh as the seed of David was designated to be the
firstborn Son of God. Before His incarnation, Christ, the divine
One, was already the Son of God (John 1:18; Rom. 8:3). By incarnation He put on an element, the human flesh, which had nothing to do with divinity; that part of Him needed to be sanctified
and uplifted by passing through death and resurrection. By resurrection His human nature was sanctified, uplifted, and transformed. Hence, by resurrection He was designated the Son of God
with His humanity (Acts 13:33; Heb. 1:5). His resurrection was
His designation.

In His death Christ's humanity was crucified. When Christ
was crucified on the cross, His humanity was crucified there. First
Peter 3:18 says, "Christ...on the one hand being put to death in

the flesh, but on the other, made alive in the Spirit." Here we can see that...when Christ was on the cross, while His flesh was being put to death, His divinity was actively working.

Then, in the resurrection of Christ, His crucified humanity was made alive by the Spirit of His divinity and was uplifted into the sonship of the only begotten Son of God. For example, a grain of wheat falls into the ground and dies. That death causes the shell of the grain to be broken and destroyed, yet at the same time, the life within the grain is made active...and begins to germinate and grow. This germination, this growth, is resurrection. ...When a grain of wheat is buried in the ground, is it dying or living? If the grain of wheat were merely dying, no farmer would want to sow any grain. Everyone who sows knows that although a grain dies alone when it is sown, it brings forth thirty grains, sixty grains, and even a hundred grains.

John 12:24 says, "Unless the grain of wheat falls into the ground and dies, it abides alone; but if it dies, it bears much fruit." To bear much fruit is to be made alive, and this takes place at the time of dying. The grain of wheat, on the one hand, is dying, but on the other hand, is being made alive. The same is true with Christ when He was on the cross. Although His humanity, His flesh, as His outer shell, was crucified on the cross, the Spirit as the essence of His divinity was greatly activated so that His crucified humanity might be made alive in resurrection. Not only so, when His humanity was made alive, it was uplifted into the sonship of the only begotten Son of God. In other words, as soon as He was resurrected, His humanity was uplifted into the divine sonship. Thus, He was begotten to be the firstborn Son of God. (*How to Be a Co-worker and an Elder and How to Fulfill Their Obligations,* pp. 28-30)

Further Reading: How to Be a Co-worker and an Elder and How to Fulfill Their Obligations, ch. 2; The Practical Way to Live a Life according to the High Peak of the Divine Revelation in the Holy Scriptures, ch. 3

Enlightenment and inspiration: _____

_____

_____

_____

Morning Nourishment

John But this He said concerning the Spirit, whom those
7:39 who believed into Him were about to receive; for *the*
Spirit was not yet, because Jesus had not yet been
glorified.

Phil. For I know that for me this will turn out to salvation
1:19 through your petition and *the* bountiful supply of
the Spirit of Jesus Christ.

The second great thing accomplished by Christ in the stage
of His inclusion was that He became the life-giving Spirit (1 Cor.
15:45b). In His resurrection, not only was He begotten to be the
firstborn Son of God, but also as the last Adam in the flesh He
became the life-giving Spirit. Christ's being the last Adam
means that after Him there is no more Adam. In Christ, Adam
was ended. In resurrection Christ as the last Adam in the flesh
became the life-giving Spirit.

First Corinthians 15:45b says, "The last Adam [Christ in the
flesh] became a life-giving Spirit." First, in His incarnation,
Christ became flesh for accomplishing redemption. Then in His
resurrection, Christ, the last Adam, became the life-giving Spirit
for dispensing life.

John 7:39 says, "...For the Spirit was not yet, because Jesus
had not yet been glorified."...Jesus was glorified when He was
resurrected (Luke 24:26). Before He was resurrected, that is,
before He was glorified, the Spirit of God was not the life-giving
Spirit. Before the resurrection of Christ, the Spirit of God could
move upon the face of the waters, could contact people, and could
sanctify people, but He could not impart life into people, because
He was not yet the life-giving Spirit. The title *the Spirit of life*
was not mentioned until Romans 8:2. Therefore, prior to the resurrection of Christ, *the Spirit was not yet* means that there was
not yet the life-giving Spirit. (*How to Be a Co-worker and an
Elder and How to Fulfill Their Obligations,* pp. 30-32)

Today's Reading

Christ, the Son of God as the second of the Divine Trinity,

after completing His ministry on the earth, became (was transfigured into) the life-giving Spirit in His resurrection. In the pre-
vious stage Christ was a man in the flesh, but after He had
entered into resurrection, He was transfigured into a life-giving
Spirit.

This life-giving Spirit is signified by the water that flowed out
of the pierced side of Jesus on the cross (John 19:34). The four
Gospels all give a record of the death of the Lord Jesus, but only
John tells us that blood and water flowed out from His pierced
side. The blood signifies redemption, and the water signifies life-
imparting. Christ as the life-giving Spirit is signified by the water.

Furthermore, through His death on the cross, Christ
released the divine life that was confined in the shell of His
humanity and dispensed it into His believers to make them the
many members which constitute His Body (John 12:24). When
Christ was in His flesh, His divine life was held and confined in
the shell of His flesh. This can be illustrated by a grain of wheat.
Unless the grain of wheat is sown into the ground and dies, the
life within the grain is confined within its shell. But when the
grain is sown into the ground and dies, the shell of the grain is
broken and the life within is released.

This life-giving Spirit, who is the pneumatic Christ, is also
called the Spirit of life (Rom. 8:2), the Spirit of Jesus (Acts 16:7),
the Spirit of Christ (Rom. 8:9), the Spirit of Jesus Christ (Phil.
1:19), and the Lord Spirit (2 Cor. 3:18).

Here, we are speaking about "the pneumatic Christ," not "the
spiritual Christ." "The pneumatic Christ" means that Christ is
the Spirit....This pneumatic Christ, who is the Spirit of life, the
Spirit of Jesus, the Spirit of Christ, the Spirit of Jesus Christ,
and the Lord Spirit, supplies our needs in every way that we
may gradually grow in His life and nature unto maturity. (*How
to Be a Co-worker and an Elder and How to Fulfill Their Obligations,* pp. 32-33)

Further Reading: The Divine and Mystical Realm, chs. 1, 3

Enlightenment and inspiration: _____
_____
_____
_____

Morning Nourishment

1 Pet. **Blessed be the God and Father of our Lord Jesus**
1:3 **Christ, who according to His great mercy has regen-**
erated us unto a living hope through the resurrec-
tion of Jesus Christ from the dead.
1 Cor. **For also in one Spirit we were all baptized into one**
12:13 **Body, whether Jews or Greeks, whether slaves or**
free, and were all given to drink one Spirit.

The third great thing accomplished by Christ in the stage of
His inclusion was that He regenerated the believers for His Body
(1 Pet. 1:3)....The purpose of Christ's being begotten to be the firstborn Son of God and becoming the life-giving Spirit was to regener-
ate the believers that they may become the many sons of God, born
of God with Him....Therefore, the birth of Christ in resurrection
was indeed a big delivery,...giving birth to millions of sons of God.
The first One was the firstborn Son, Christ, and the rest were the
many sons, all the believers belonging to Christ. This is for the
composition of the house of God, even the household of God. This
is also for the constitution of the Body of Christ to be His fullness
...to consummate the eternal expression and expansion of the
processed and consummated Triune God. (*How to Be a Co-worker
and an Elder and How to Fulfill Their Obligations,* pp. 33-34)

Today's Reading

In one Spirit all the believers have been baptized into the one
Body of Christ [1 Cor. 12:13]. This one Spirit is Christ Himself. In
Him as the one Spirit we all have been baptized into one Body. At
the same time, all the believers who were baptized in the one
Spirit have been given to drink this Spirit.

To be baptized is to enter into the one Spirit, whereas to drink
is to receive the one Spirit into us....We have been baptized into
Christ as the life-giving Spirit—this is "the Spirit enveloping us."
Furthermore, we have been given to drink the Spirit—this is "us
enveloping the Spirit." Consequently, we have the Spirit within
and without. Thus, in this Spirit, we all become one organic
entity—the Body of Christ.

In His resurrection Christ gave Himself as the all-inclusive, life-giving Spirit without measure through His speaking of the words of God (John 3:34)....When you receive the words of God and the words of God enter into you, you have the Spirit. In John 6:63 the Lord told us, "The words which I have spoken to you are spirit and are life." Once we receive the words of God into us, these words that are in us become spirit and life. Therefore, when the Lord speaks to us, He gives us life and the Spirit without measure. I truly can testify that the more I receive the Lord's words, the more I am filled with the Spirit, even without measure.

Christ regenerated the believers for His Body that all the believers in Christ may be built up into a dwelling place of God in their spirit indwelt by Him as the Spirit (Eph. 2:22). Here, to be built up is to be constituted together. We are being built up into a dwelling place of God in our spirit indwelt by Him as the Spirit. Ultimately, this dwelling place is the New Jerusalem (Rev. 21:3).

Such a constitution, such a building, is consummated through dispositional sanctification (Rom. 15:16), renewing (Titus 3:5), transformation (2 Cor. 3:18), and conformation (Rom. 8:29). After regenerating us, God sanctifies us in our disposition, renews us in our old creation, and transforms us in our entire being. Not only so, He conforms us to the image of His firstborn Son that all of us may be God's sons in life and nature and, with His firstborn Son, become God's corporate son as God's expression, God's expansion. The New Jerusalem is such a corporate expression, expansion, and enlargement of God. The Bible begins with "In the beginning God..." (Gen. 1:1). At that time, the unique God was "alone." However, at the end, the Bible mentions a city, the New Jerusalem. This city is not simple, requiring the explanation of the Bible with sixty-six books. This is because this city, the New Jerusalem, is the enlarged God. (*How to Be a Co-worker and an Elder and How to Fulfill Their Obligations,* pp. 34-36)

Further Reading: How to Be a Co-worker and an Elder and How to Fulfill Their Obligations, ch. 2

Enlightenment and inspiration: _____
_____
_____
_____

Morning Nourishment

Psa. Jehovah is my Shepherd; I will lack nothing.
23:1-2 He makes me lie down in green pastures; He leads
me beside waters of rest.
  3 He restores my soul; He guides me on the paths of
righteousness for His name's sake.
  4 Even though I walk through the valley of the
shadow of death, I do not fear evil, for You are with
me; Your rod and Your staff, they comfort me.
  5 You spread a table before me in the presence of my
adversaries; You anoint my head with oil; my cup
runs over.
  6 Surely goodness and lovingkindness will follow me
all the days of my life, and I will dwell in the house of
Jehovah for the length of *my* days.

John 21 is the completion and consummation of the Gospel of
John,…showing that Christ's heavenly ministry and the apostles'
ministry on the earth cooperate together to carry out God's New
Testament economy.…After His resurrection and before His
ascension,…[the Lord] commissioned Peter to feed His lambs and
shepherd His sheep…(John 21:15-17). Shepherding implies feeding, but it includes much more than feeding. To shepherd is to
take all-inclusive tender care of the flock.…This is to incorporate
the apostolic ministry with Christ's heavenly ministry to take
care of God's flock, which is the church that issues in the Body of
Christ. (*Crystallization-study of the Gospel of John,* pp. 130-131)

Today's Reading

Psalm 23…tells us that Christ's shepherding of us is in five
stages.…The resurrected Christ shepherds us first in the initial
stage of enjoyment in green pastures and at waters of rest (Psa.
23:1-2).…The little lamb lying down in the pasture and eating the
grass does not have to worry about proper table manners. This is
just like an infant lying in the bosom of his nursing mother.

He also leads us to waters of rest (Psa. 23:2b; 1 Cor. 12:13b).
The green pastures are Christ, and the waters of rest are the

Spirit. The Spirit is the restful waters. When we go to take care of the new ones, we must not only feed them with Christ but also help them to drink of the Spirit. We must help them to call on the name of the Lord and to pray. This is to help them to drink the Spirit by exercising their spirit.

Psalm 23:3 [indicates]…the second stage of revival and transformation on the paths of righteousness. To restore our soul is to revive us. Restoring also includes renewing and transforming.… He restores us—revives and transforms us—in our soul to make us take His way, to walk on the paths of righteousness.

The third stage is the stage of the experience of the presence of the resurrected pneumatic Christ through the valley of the shadow of death (Psa. 23:4). Even though we walk through the valley of the shadow of death, we do not fear evil, for the pneumatic Christ is with us (2 Tim. 4:22).…His presence is a comfort, a rescue, and a sustaining power to us when we are walking in the valley of the shadow of death.

The fourth stage [is] the deeper and higher enjoyment of the resurrected Christ (Psa. 23:5). The Lord spreads a table—a feast—before us in the presence of our adversaries (1 Cor. 10:21). The Lord's table is a feast.…We need to fight the battle in the Lord all week long before we come to the Lord's table. Then we will be able to have a rich enjoyment of the Lord as our feast at His table.

Psalm 23:6 speaks of the fifth stage of the lifelong enjoyment of the divine goodness and kindness in the house of Jehovah. Surely goodness and kindness will follow us (the grace of Christ and the love of God will be with us—2 Cor. 13:14) all the days of our life (in the present age),…[and] we will dwell in the house of Jehovah (the church and the New Jerusalem—1 Tim. 3:15-16; Rev. 21:2-3, 22) for the length of our days (in the present age and in the coming age and in eternity). (*Life-study of the Psalms,* pp. 139-141, 144-147)

Further Reading: Crystallization-study of the Gospel of John, msg. 13; *Life-study of the Psalms,* msg. 11; *How to Be a Co-worker and an Elder and How to Fulfill Their Obligations,* ch. 6

Enlightenment and inspiration: _____
_____
_____
_____

Hymns, #242

1   The Spirit of God today
     The Spirit of Jesus is,
     The God-man who died and rose,
     Ascending to glory His.

2   'Tis from such a Jesus came
     The Spirit of Jesus to us,
     To make His reality
     Experience unto us.

3   The Spirit of Jesus has
     All elements human, divine,
     The living of man in Him
     And glory of God combine.

4   The suff'ring of human life,
     Effectiveness of His death,
     His rising and reigning too
     Are all in the Spirit's breath.

5   With all these components true
     His Spirit in us doth move,
     And by His anointing full
     The riches of Christ we prove.

6   This Spirit of Jesus doth
     Encompass both great and small;
     Inclusively He doth work
     In us, making God our all.

Composition for prophecy with main point and sub-points: _____

_____

_____

_____

_____

_____

_____

_____

_____

_____

_____

_____

_____

_____

_____

_____

_____

_____

_____

_____

_____

_____

_____

_____

_____

_____

_____

_____

_____

_____

_____

_____

_____

_____

_____

_____

_____

_____

_____

Experiencing Christ
in the Stage of Intensification
as the Sevenfold Intensified
Life-giving Spirit

Scripture Reading: Rev. 1:4-5; 3:1; 4:5; 5:6

Day 1 I. Revelation is a book of administration (4:2, 5; 5:6), intensification (1:4; 3:1; 4:5; 5:6), and consummation (21:1-2; 22:1-2, 17).

II. The Christ in the book of Revelation is a "different" Christ from the One revealed in the Gospels; in 1:13-18 He is a "fierce" Christ.

III. Because of the degradation of the church caused by leaven (Matt. 13:33), the winds of teaching (Eph. 4:14), and the leaving of the first love (Rev. 2:4-5), Christ as the life-giving Spirit has been intensified sevenfold to become the seven Spirits—the sevenfold intensified life-giving Spirit (1 Cor. 15:45b; Rev. 1:4; 3:1; 4:5; 5:6):

Day 2 A. The title *the seven Spirits* indicates that the Spirit has been intensified sevenfold (1:4).

B. The seven Spirits are the sevenfold intensified Spirit, typified by the seven lamps on the lampstand (Exo. 25:31, 37; Zech. 4:2, 10; 3:9).

C. At the time the book of Revelation was written, the church had become degraded, and the age was dark; therefore, the sevenfold intensified Spirit of God was needed for God's move and work on earth.

D. The Lord reacted to the degradation of the church by intensifying Himself sevenfold to become the sevenfold intensified life-giving Spirit (Rev. 4:5; 5:6).

E. Seven is the number for completion in God's move, God's operation (v. 1; 6:1; 8:1-2; 16:1).

F. The number seven also signifies intensification (Isa. 30:26; Dan. 3:19):

   1. Since the life-giving Spirit has been inten-
       sified sevenfold, all the elements of the
       Spirit have been intensified sevenfold for
       our experience (Rom. 8:2; Heb. 10:29).
   2. Today the Spirit, who is filling us and satu-
       rating us to save us organically, is the
       sevenfold intensified life-giving Spirit
       (Rom. 5:10; Rev. 3:1; 5:6).

Day 3 **IV. Revelation 1:4-5 reveals the Divine Trinity—
       the One who is and who was and who is com-
       ing, the seven Spirits, and Jesus Christ:**
   A. The Trinity in 1:4-5 is the economical Trinity,
       for here we see the administration, the move,
       and the work of the Trinity (4:5; 5:6).
   B. The seven Spirits are undoubtedly the one
       Spirit of God (Eph. 4:4), because they are ranked
       in the Godhead in Revelation 1:4-5.
   C. In essence and existence the Spirit is one, but in
       function and work the Spirit is seven (Eph. 4:4;
       Rev. 1:4).
   D. In 1:4-5 the Spirit becomes the second, the cen-
       ter, of the Divine Trinity:
       1. This reveals the importance of the inten-
           sified function of the sevenfold Spirit of
           God.
       2. This also signifies the crucial need of the
           Spirit for God's move to counteract the degra-
           dation of the church (2:4, 14, 20; 3:1, 15-17).

Day 4 **V. Christ has the seven Spirits of God and the
       seven stars (v. 1a):**
   A. The seven Spirits are the means for Christ to
       speak to the church in Sardis, a dying church;
       a dying church needs Christ to make it living
       through the seven Spirits (v. 1b).
   B. Revelation 3:1 implies that the seven Spirits are
       for the seven stars, the leading ones; in order to
       be a star taking the lead in the church, we need
       the sevenfold intensified Spirit.

   VI. The seven Spirits of God are the seven lamps

of fire burning before the administrating throne of God (4:5):

A. The seven lamps of fire burning before God's throne indicate that the seven Spirits are for the carrying out of God's administration and are related to His economy and move (1:4):
   1. The seven lamps of fire before the throne of God are for enlightening, searching, exposing, judging, and burning.
   2. God is administrating His government by enlightening, searching, exposing, judging, and burning (1 Pet. 4:12, 17).
   3. The seven lamps will burn everything that does not correspond to God's nature but will refine those things that are according to His nature (1:7).

Day 5   B. Eventually, in our experience the burning lamps of fire become the flow of living water; the seven lamps become one river (Dan. 7:9-10; Rev. 4:5; 22:1):
   1. In 4:5 we have the seven lamps burning before the throne of God; in 22:1 we have the river of water of life proceeding out of the throne of God.
   2. According to our experience, after we receive the burning of the seven lamps, the seven Spirits become one flow of living water.
   3. The Spirit never fails to flow after He burns us; His flowing always follows His burning.

Day 6   **VII. The seven Spirits of God are the seven eyes of the Lamb (5:6):**

A. In the economical Trinity in Revelation, the second of the Godhead is the seven Spirits and becomes the seven eyes of the third of the Trinity (1:4-5).

B. In God's administration Christ needs the seven Spirits to be His eyes; the way that Christ carries out God's economy is by the seven Spirits as His eyes (5:1-7).

C. The seven eyes of Christ, which are the seven Spirits of God, are Christ's expression in God's move for God's building.

D. The seven eyes of the Lamb are for watching, observing, and transfusing (v. 6):

1. Christ as the redeeming Lamb has seven observing and searching eyes for executing God's judgment upon the universe to fulfill His eternal purpose, which will consummate in the building up of the New Jerusalem (21:2).

2. The seven Spirits as the seven eyes of the Lamb transfuse all that the Lamb is into our being so that we may be the same as He is (1 John 3:1).

3. Christ's eyes are upon us so that we may be transformed and conformed into His image for God's building (Zech. 3:9; Rom. 12:2; 8:29; 2 Cor. 3:18).

Morning Nourishment

Rev. And in the midst of the lampstands One like the Son of
1:13-16 Man, clothed with a garment reaching to the feet, and
girded about at the breasts with a golden girdle. And
His head and hair were as white as white wool, as
snow; and His eyes were like a flame of fire; and His
feet were like shining bronze, as having been fired in
a furnace; and His voice was like the sound of many
waters. And He had in His right hand seven stars; and
out of His mouth proceeded a sharp two-edged sword;
and His face *shone* as the sun shines in its power.

3:1 And to the messenger of the church in Sardis write:
These things says He who has the seven Spirits of
God and the seven stars...

The Christ in Revelation is a "different" Christ from that in
the four Gospels. I do not believe in another Christ, but I do
believe in a "different" Christ. The Christ in the four Gospels had
only two eyes, but the Christ in Revelation has seven eyes....In
the four Gospels words of grace are proceeding out of His mouth
(Luke 4:22), but in Revelation a sharp two-edged sword is proceeding out of His mouth [Rev. 1:16].

In the four Gospels, John was reclining on Jesus' bosom (John
13:23). In the book of Revelation, however, when John saw such a
Christ he fell at His feet as dead; he was full of fear (1:17). Christ
as the High Priest in Revelation 1 also holds seven stars in His
right hand (v. 20) and His feet are like "shining bronze, as having
been fired in a furnace" (v. 15). Revelation 1:14 also tells us that
"His head and hair were as white as white wool, as snow." Proba-
bly in our past none of us ever heard a sermon that Christ, our
Redeemer, has seven eyes and His eyes are as a flame of fire
(1:14)....We all need to see the vision concerning Christ in Revelation 1. (*God's New Testament Economy,* p. 208)

Today's Reading

The third section of [Christ's ministry is] His sevenfold
intensified heavenly ministry...carried out by Him sevenfold

intensified organically in the mystical realm as the Christ, as the sevenfold intensified life-giving Spirit, from the degradation of the church to the coming of the new heaven and new earth. The degradation of the church began within the first century. In 2 Timothy Paul told us that all in Asia had turned away from him, leaving his ministry (1:15). Also, ones like Hymenaeus and Philetus were trying to overthrow the truth concerning the resurrection, saying the resurrection had already taken place (2:17-18). Paul mentioned Demas abandoning him because of his love for the present age (4:10). He also spoke of Alexander the coppersmith doing many evil things to him (4:14)....All these descriptions show us the degradation of the church. Shortly after writing 2 Timothy around A.D. 67, Paul was martyred. Less than thirty years later, John wrote the book of Revelation which shows the degradation of the churches. He also wrote 2 John, which is an Epistle revealing the prohibition against heresy, which was already creeping into the church.

The book of Revelation opens in this way: "Grace to you and peace from Him who is and who was and who is coming, and from the seven Spirits who are before His throne, and from Jesus Christ, the faithful Witness, the Firstborn of the dead, and the Ruler of the kings of the earth" (1:4-5). In these verses the seven Spirits are listed as the second of the Divine Trinity. Then the book of Revelation gives us a full record of the move of the sevenfold Spirit in Christ's heavenly ministry to do a number of things.

The sevenfold intensified Spirit worked to save the believers in the church in Ephesus from the formal church life, which had lost the first love to the Lord, the shining capacity of the lampstand, and the enjoyment of Christ as life, to become overcomers so that they would be rewarded to eat of the tree of life in the Paradise of God—the New Jerusalem in the kingdom age (Rev. 2:1-7). (*The Divine and Mystical Realm*, pp. 72-73)

Further Reading: Incarnation, Inclusion, and Intensification, ch. 1; *The Divine and Mystical Realm*, ch. 5

Enlightenment and inspiration: _____

_____

_____

Morning Nourishment

Rev. And out of the throne come forth lightnings and
4:5 voices and thunders. And *there were* seven lamps of
     fire burning before the throne, which are the seven
     Spirits of God.
5:6 And I saw in the midst of the throne...a Lamb stand-
     ing as having *just* been slain, having seven horns
     and seven eyes, which are the seven Spirits of God
     sent forth into all the earth.

In the book of Revelation the Spirit is called the seven Spirits
(1:4; 4:5; 5:6)....The seven Spirits in Revelation 1:4 undoubtedly
are the Spirit of God because They are ranked among the Triune
God. As seven is the number for completion in God's operation, so
the seven Spirits must be for God's move on earth. In substance
and existence God's Spirit is one. In the intensified function and
work of God's operation His Spirit is sevenfold. It is like the lampstand....In existence it is one lampstand, but in function it is seven
lamps. At the time the book of Revelation was written, the church
had become degraded, and the age was dark. Therefore, the sevenfold intensified Spirit of God was needed for God's move on earth.

In Matthew 28:19 the sequence of the Triune God is the
Father, the Son, and the Holy Spirit. But in Revelation 1:4 and 5
the sequence is changed. The seven Spirits of God are listed in the
second place instead of the third. This reveals the importance of
the intensified function of the sevenfold Spirit of God. This point
is confirmed by the repeated emphasis on the Spirit's speaking in
2:7, 11, 17, 29; 3:6, 13, 22; 14:13; and 22:17.

The title "the seven Spirits" indicates that the Spirit has been
intensified sevenfold. This Spirit intensifies all the elements of
the Spirit: divinity, incarnation, crucifixion, resurrection, reality,
life, and grace. (*The Conclusion of the New Testament,* p. 867)

Today's Reading

Shortly after the church was produced, it began to become degraded....Eventually the church degraded to such an extent that
the Lord could no longer tolerate it, and He reacted by intensifying

Himself sevenfold to become the sevenfold intensified Spirit (Rev. 1:4; 5:6). He became intensified sevenfold to deal with the degradation of the church. (*Incarnation, Inclusion, and Intensification,* p. 18)

Christians often say that Christ's ministry is of two parts or sections—His earthly ministry and His heavenly ministry. However, Christ's ministry is actually of three sections. The third section of His ministry is the sevenfold intensified heavenly ministry. This ministry is still His heavenly ministry, but it is a heavenly ministry that has been intensified sevenfold.

Very few Christians realize that today we should not be merely in Christ's heavenly ministry but in His sevenfold intensified heavenly ministry. We all need to be in the third section of Christ's ministry. Today the Lord is working not only as the life-giving Spirit but also as the sevenfold intensified Spirit. This Spirit may be compared to the shining of the sun spoken of in Isaiah 30:26, which says that in the millennium "the light of the sun will be sevenfold." Today the Spirit who is filling us and saturating us is the sevenfold intensified life-giving Spirit. We all need to see this and then pray, "Lord, I worship You that You are working in me as the sevenfold intensified Spirit."

In the past some have tried to argue with us, saying that Christ cannot change and quoting Hebrews 13:8, which says, "Jesus Christ is the same yesterday and today, yes, even forever." Regarding this we would point out that Christ has not changed essentially, but He has changed economically. Essentially He is the same from eternity to eternity, but economically He has changed in three ways—by becoming flesh in His incarnation, by becoming the life-giving Spirit in His resurrection, and by intensifying Himself to be the sevenfold intensified life-giving Spirit in His intensification. (*The Secret of God's Organic Salvation—"The Spirit Himself with Our Spirit,"* pp. 79-80)

Further Reading: The Conclusion of the New Testament, msg. 80; The Secret of God's Organic Salvation—"The Spirit Himself with Our Spirit," ch. 6

Enlightenment and inspiration: _____
_____
_____
_____

Morning Nourishment

Rev. John to the seven churches which are in Asia: Grace
1:4-5 to you and peace from Him who is and who was and
who is coming, and from the seven Spirits who are
before His throne, and from Jesus Christ, the faithful Witness, the Firstborn of the dead, and the Ruler
of the kings of the earth. To Him who loves us and
has released us from our sins by His blood.
3:22 He who has an ear, let him hear what the Spirit says
to the churches.

In God's existence, the Father, the Son, and the Spirit coexist
and coinhere from eternity to eternity. There is no modifier
needed for the essential Trinity. The book of Revelation, however,
does not touch the existence of the Trinity but the economy of the
Trinity. According to God's economy the Father is the One who is
now, who was in the past, and who shall be in the future. These
modifiers indicate economy. Also, in God's existence, the Spirit of
God is one, but in God's economy the Spirit of God is seven in function. Essentially God's Spirit in existence is one, but economically
God's Spirit has to be intensified to fulfill His function to carry out
God's economy. In essence God the Son is just the Son, but in
God's economy He is Jesus, Christ, the faithful Witness, the Firstborn of the dead, the Ruler of the kings of the earth, the One who
loves us and has loosed us from our sins by His blood, the One
who has made us a kingdom, priests to His God and Father, and
the One who comes to execute God's final government....The
sequence of every modifier of the Son in Revelation 1:5-7 is
related to God's move, God's economy. (*God's New Testament
Economy*, p. 212)

Today's Reading

In God's essence, the Trinity is simply the Father, the Son, and
the Spirit. In God's economy, though, the Trinity is complicated.
Also, in God's essence the Father is first, the Son is second, and
the Spirit is third. In God's economy, however, the Spirit comes
before God the Son. The Spirit carries out God's administration

and infuses and searches the churches. In the four Gospels, the Son was more present than the Spirit, but in Revelation the Spirit is more present than the Son, so the Spirit comes before the Son in the sequence of the economical Trinity in Revelation 1. The Trinity in Matthew 28 is the Trinity of God's existence, the essential Trinity, and the Trinity in Revelation is the Trinity in God's economy, the economical Trinity.

The Father was working in eternity, He was working in creation, He was working in the Son for redemption, and He shall be working. This shows us that the title "Him who is, and who was, and who is coming" does not mainly refer to existence, but to the Father's working, the activities of the Father, in different times. The Father works in the past, He works today, and He will work in the future.

The seven Spirits are undoubtedly the Spirit of God, because they are ranked among the Triune God in Revelation 1:4 and 5. As seven is the number for completion in God's operation, so the seven Spirits must be for God's move on the earth. In substance and existence God's Spirit is one; in the intensified function and work of God's operation, God's Spirit is sevenfold....At the time this book was written, the church had become degraded; the age was dark. Therefore, the sevenfold intensified Spirit of God was needed for God's move and work on the earth.

The seven Spirits of God are listed in the second place instead of the third. This reveals the importance of the intensified function of the sevenfold Spirit of God. This point is confirmed by the repeated emphasis on the Spirit's speaking in 2:7, 11, 17, 29; 3:6, 13, 22; 14:13; 22:17. At the opening of the other Epistles, only the Father and the Son are mentioned, from whom grace and peace are given to the receivers. Here, however, the Spirit is also included....This also signifies the crucial need for the Spirit for God's move to counteract the degradation of the church. (*God's New Testament Economy,* pp. 213, 210-211)

Further Reading: God's New Testament Economy, chs. 20-21

Enlightenment and inspiration: _____

_____

_____

Morning Nourishment

1 Pet. Beloved, do not think that the fiery ordeal among
4:12 you, coming to you for a trial, is strange, as if *it were* a
strange thing happening to you.
17 For it is time for the judgment to begin from the
house of God...
1:7 So that the proving of your faith, much more pre-
cious than of gold which perishes though it is proved
by fire, may be found unto praise and glory and honor
at the revelation of Jesus Christ.

The sevenfold intensified Spirit of God meets the need of the degraded churches....Revelation 3:1 speaks of "He who has the seven Spirits of God and the seven stars." This is Christ as the One who takes care of the church. He spoke to the church in Sardis, a dying church. Such a dying church needed such a Christ to make it living through the seven Spirits. This verse also implies that the seven Spirits are for the seven stars. The seven stars are the leading ones. To be a star taking the lead in the church, you need the sevenfold Spirit. (*The Spirit,* pp. 106-107)

Today's Reading

The lampstand has seven lamps, and these seven lamps are the Spirit for the expression of the Triune God. The lampstand has three aspects: the gold essence, the form, and the expression. The essence is the Father, the form is the Son, and the expression is the Spirit. Zechariah 4 reveals that the seven lamps refer to the Spirit. Then in Revelation 4:5 the seven lamps of fire burning before God's throne are the seven Spirits of God. The seven lamps of the lampstand are the seven Spirits before the throne of God to execute God's administration on the whole earth.

In Revelation 5:6 the Spirit is symbolized by the seven eyes of the Lamb, which are the seven Spirits of God sent forth into all the earth. The seven eyes of the Lamb are also the seven lamps of the lampstand. The lamps are for enlightening and burning; the eyes are for watching and observing and also for infusing and transfusing...for the carrying out of God's administration. These seven eyes are…transfusing all that the Lamb is into our being so that we may become the same as He is. Today the seven Spirits are moving to accomplish God's building for the fulfillment of His New Testament economy. (*The Spirit,* p. 39)

God will touch the earth by the seven lamps, by His seven Spirits, which are burning, shining, observing, searching, and judging. …In Exodus 25 and Zechariah 4 the seven lamps, signifying the enlightening of the Spirit of God in God's move, are for God's building. In Revelation 4:5 the seven lamps are for God's judgment, which will issue in the building of the New Jerusalem. While God executes His judgment, His sevenfold intensified Spirit will carry out His eternal building by searching, enlightening, and judging.

Today, God is administrating His government by means of enlightening, searching, exposing, judging, and burning. Anything that does not correspond to God's nature will be burned by His fire. Although we have been saved and have undergone some amount of transformation, our work will be burned if it is wood, grass, and stubble and not gold, silver, and precious stones (1 Cor. 3:15). Any fleshly work, work done in the name of the Lord but actually having nothing to do with Him, will be burned. Everything that is not of God or according to God will be counted by God as wood, grass, and stubble, and it will be burned by fire. This burning is the carrying out of God's administration. The Bible reveals that God is the burning One (Deut. 4:24; Heb. 12:29). All things outside of Him or that do not correspond to His nature will be burned.

Although the seven enlightening, searching, exposing, judging, and burning lamps will burn all that does not correspond to God, they will refine those things that are truly according to His nature. The dross will go to the lake of fire, but the refined gold will go to the New Jerusalem. (*The Conclusion of the New Testament,* pp. 886-887)

Further Reading: The Ultimate Significance of the Golden Lampstand, chs. 4-5; *The Spirit,* ch. 10

Enlightenment and inspiration: _____

_____

_____

Morning Nourishment

Dan. I watched until thrones were set, and the Ancient of
7:9-10 Days sat down. His clothing was like white snow, and
the hair of His head was like pure wool; His throne
was flames of fire, its wheels, burning fire. A stream
of fire issued forth and came out from before Him....
Rev. And he showed me a river of water of life, bright as
22:1 crystal, proceeding out of the throne of God and of
the Lamb in the middle of its street.

Eventually, the seven lamps before the throne become the
river of life proceeding out of the throne. In Revelation 4 we have
the seven lamps burning before the throne of God, and in chapter
twenty-two we have the river of water of life proceeding out of the
throne of God. Thus, the seven lamps become one river. According to
our experience, the seven Spirits of God are firstly the seven burning
lamps. After we receive the burning of the seven lamps, the seven
Spirits become one flow. In chapter four we do not yet have the New
Jerusalem, for with only the seven lamps there is no building.
However, when we see the river proceeding out of the throne to
replace the seven lamps, we know that the building has also come.
Perhaps yesterday you were under the enlightening and the burning of the seven lamps. But this morning you are in the flow of the
water of life. With only the lamps, there was no building; but with
the flow, there is the New Jerusalem. When we are in the flow, we
are a part of God's building. (*Life-study of Revelation,* p. 781)

Today's Reading

According to the book of Revelation, the seven Spirits of God are
firstly the lamps burning before God's administrative throne. Eventually, in God's building, these seven Spirits of God become the river
of water of life proceeding from the throne. Now this throne is not
only the administrative throne, but also the supplying throne. In
this way we have the building. The more we are enlightened and
receive the burning, the more we are in the flow of life, and the more
we are in the flow of life, the more we are built up. This is the way to
experience the building. (*Life-study of Revelation,* pp. 781-782)

The Spirit never fails to flow after He burns in us; His flowing always follows His burning. Whether there is more burning after the flowing depends on whether there is anything more in us that needs burning. The burning will go on until everything is burned away. If one day we do not become angry, regardless of how others treat us, then we need no further burning,...[and] there is only the flowing. When we reach this stage, we are the New Jerusalem. ...In the New Jerusalem...there will be no more burning, because the burning Spirit has become the flowing Spirit. There will be a river of water of life, bright as crystal, flowing to eternity.

None among us has reached such a stage, but thank the Lord, we are on the way....It is only when we enter into these subjective experiences that we have first the seven shining lamps, then the seven lamps of fire, and then...a river of water of life flowing in us for us to be watered, saturated, and supplied and for us to supply others. This is the reality in the church. Today, the church in a proper condition is the New Jerusalem. Some of us are...still in Revelation 4 with lightnings, voices, thunders, and seven lamps of fire burning before the throne....Chapter four is not the end but the process; the end is in Revelation 21 and 22....[There], the throne in chapter four reappears. It is still the same throne, but what proceeds from it is not fire but a flow.

Today in the church we...should have not only the lamps shining and the fire burning but also the living water flowing. When fire is needed, there is fire, and when water is needed, there is water, but fire is not the goal; it is the procedure. Water is the goal. The ultimate goal of the church is that people are brought into the flow of the living water. "The Spirit and the bride say, Come! And let him who hears say, Come! And let him who is thirsty come; let him who wills take the water of life freely" (Rev. 22:17). This is salvation, this is the gospel, and this is the church life. (*The Ultimate Significance of the Golden Lampstand,* pp. 86-87)

Further Reading: Life-study of Revelation, msg. 68; *The Ultimate Significance of the Golden Lampstand,* ch. 6

Enlightenment and inspiration: _____
_____
_____
_____

Morning Nourishment

Rom. And do not be fashioned according to this age, but be
12:2 transformed by the renewing of the mind that you
      may prove what the will of God is, that which is good
      and well pleasing and perfect.
8:29 Because those whom He foreknew, He also predesti-
      nated *to be* conformed to the image of His Son, that
      He might be the Firstborn among many brothers.
Rev. And I saw the holy city, New Jerusalem, coming down
21:2 out of heaven from God, prepared as a bride adorned
      for her husband.

The traditional teaching of the Divine Trinity stresses that the
Father, the Son, and the Spirit are three separate persons. The
last book of the Bible, however, shows us that the Spirit has
become the eyes of the Son. We cannot say that the eyes of a person are another person. This shows that the traditional teaching
of the Divine Trinity is short of the adequate and full knowledge
of the Bible. Economically speaking, the Spirit of God in God's
administration is the eyes of the administrating Son. This is for
function, not for existence. In order for us to do anything we need
our eyes. This shows us that, in the divine administration, Christ
needs the Spirit to be His eyes.

In order to carry out His administration God needs an executor and this Executor is this wonderful Person, the slain Lamb.
The all-inclusive, excellent, marvelous, mysterious, and wonderful One is the Executor of God's administration. John saw the view
that in the entire universe no one was qualified or worthy to carry
out God's administration except this One (Rev. 5:4-6). Because He
is qualified and worthy, the seven seals were handed over to Him.
This One is qualified to open the seven seals, to carry out God's
economy. The way He carries out God's economy is by the seven
Spirits as His eyes. (*God's New Testament Economy,* p. 239)

Today's Reading

The seven eyes of Christ, the seven Spirits of God, are Christ's
expression in a judging way in God's move for God's building.

Even now, Christ's burning eyes are flaming over us to enlighten, search, refine, and judge us, not that we might be condemned, but that we might be purged, transformed, and conformed to His image for God's building. The Lord's judgment is motivated by love. Because He loves the church, He comes to search, enlighten, judge, refine, and purify us in order to transform us into precious stones. Eventually, this book consummates in the New Jerusalem which is built with precious materials. Where do these materials come from? They come from the seven eyes of Christ, that is, from the life-giving, transforming Spirit.

The whole Bible is related to God's building, and God's building is accomplished by the Triune God being dispensed into us. As we come to the book of Revelation, we must hold this view. If we do, we shall be able to understand this book and see that it is not mainly a book of judgment but a book for God's building.

The accomplishment of God's building requires His judgment. God's judgment is carried out by Christ's being the One with seven flaming eyes to burn, enlighten, search, purify, and refine us. Eventually, these flaming eyes infuse us with all that He is, metabolically transforming us into His being. The whole city of New Jerusalem will have the same essence and appearance as God....How can this be? Only by having the very God wrought into us. The essence of God is wrought into us by means of transfusion.

Do not ignore the seven eyes, the seven Spirits. Revelation is not a book of one Spirit; it is a book of the seven Spirits, the seven eyes of Christ, whereby the redeeming, overcoming, and building Christ transfuses Himself into all His members. While He is transfusing Himself into us, He is searching, enlightening, judging, purifying, and refining us. In this way He transforms us. How we need to see this vision! This is God's recovery today. (*Life-study of Revelation*, pp. 228-229, 269-270)

Further Reading: Life-study of Revelation, msg. 22; *God's New Testament Economy*, ch. 25

Enlightenment and inspiration: _____

_____

_____

_____

Hymns, #1122

1   "Seven Spirits" of our God—
    Lo, the age has now been turned
    To the Spirit with the Son.
    For the churches He's concerned.

      Come, O seven Spirits, come,
      Thy recovery work be done!
      Burn and search us thoroughly,
      All the churches are for Thee.
        Burn us, search us,
      All the churches are for Thee!

2   Sevenfold the Spirit is
    For the deadness of the church,
    That the saints may turn and live,
    That the Lord may burn and search.

3   Now the Spirit of our God
    Has become intensified:
    'Tis not one but sevenfold
    That the church may be supplied!

4   Now the seven Spirits are
    Seven lamps of burning fire,
    Not to teach us, but to burn,
    Satisfying God's desire.

5   See the seven Spirits now—
    Seven piercing, searching eyes.
    In the church exposing us,
    All the church He purifies.

6   Seven Spirits doth the Lord
    For the churches now employ;
    All those in the local church
    May this Spirit now enjoy.

Composition for prophecy with main point and sub-points: _____

_____

_____

_____

_____

_____

_____

_____

_____

_____

_____

_____

_____

_____

_____

_____

_____

_____

_____

_____

_____

_____

_____

_____

_____

_____

_____

_____

_____

_____

_____

_____

_____

_____

Experiencing, Enjoying, and Ministering Christ in the Stage of Intensification

Scripture Reading: Rev. 1:4; 3:1; 4:5; 5:6; 2:7, 17; 3:20; 1:2, 9; 19:10

Day 1

I. **The seven lamps of the golden lampstand are the seven Spirits as the seven lamps of fire burning before God's throne; this signifies that the seven lamps are absolutely related to God's administration, economy, and move from His throne to execute His eternal policy (Rev. 1:4; 4:5):**
   A. In order to know God's administration and economy, we must have the light of the golden lampstand from the seven shining and illumining lamps:
      1. Natural light cannot help us to know God's economy, administration, and eternal purpose; the light of the lampstand is the light in the Holy Place, which typifies the church (Matt. 5:14; 1 Cor. 1:2; Rev. 21:23, 25; 22:5).
      2. Once we enter into the realm of the church, we are enlightened to know God's eternal purpose, and we also know the path that we should take for the journey before us toward God's goal (Psa. 73:16-17).

Day 2

   B. The light of the lampstand is based on the strength of the priests' service:
      1. In 1 Samuel the lamp of God was about to go out because Eli the priest was weak and degraded (3:3).
      2. The light in the local church cannot be bright unless we fulfill our priestly duty to burn the incense and light the lamps (Exo. 25:37; 27:20-21; 30:7-8; Acts 6:4; 1 Cor. 14:24-25).

II. **The seven Spirits are the seven eyes of the redeeming Lamb and of the building stone (Rev. 4:5; 5:6; Zech. 3:9):**

A. The seven eyes are for transfusing all that Christ
is as the redeeming Lamb in His judicial redemption and as the building stone in His organic salvation into our being so that we may be saved in
His life to become exactly the same as He is for
God's building, God's expression (v. 9; 1 Pet. 2:4-5;
Rom. 5:10):

1. A person's eyes are the expression of his inner
being; transfusing is to transmit a person's
inner being into the one whom he is looking
at (2 Cor. 2:10).

2. The seven Spirits are the seven eyes by
which Christ expresses Himself; as the Lord
looks at us, His seven eyes transfuse Himself into us.

3. The church is the place where the Lord
transfuses His inner being into us for our
transformation; transformation is the
transfusing of the Lord's lovable person into
us (3:16-18; Rom. 12:2).

B. God guides us with His eyes (2 Chron. 16:9; Psa.
32:8; Prov. 15:3; 2 Cor. 2:10).

Day 3 III. **Christ as the sevenfold intensified Spirit
is working to produce the overcomers by
bringing them out of the degradation of the
church back to the enjoyment of Himself
for the finalization of God's New Testament
economy (Rev. 1:4; 3:1; 4:5; 5:6; 2:7, 17; 3:20):**

A. The overcomers love the Lord with the first love
(2:4; Col. 1:18b).

B. The overcomers enjoy eating Christ as the tree of
life in the church as today's Paradise to be a shining lampstand (Rev. 2:7; cf. v. 5).

C. The overcomers are faithful unto death in suffering poverty and trial for the crown of life (vv. 9-10).

D. The overcomers enjoy Christ as the hidden
manna, a special portion of the nourishing supply, to overcome the worldliness of the degraded
church with the idolatrous teaching of Balaam

and the hierarchical teaching of the Nicolaitans (vv. 12-17a).

Day 4

E. The overcomers are transformed to be a "white stone," justified and approved by the Lord, for the building up of the house of God, with a "new name" according to the transformation in life (v. 17b).

F. The overcomers stand strongly against the Romish teaching of Jezebel, which is full of fornication, idolatry, and the deep things of Satan (vv. 20, 24).

G. The overcomers flee spiritual death, being living in reality with nothing dying in imperfection, and they walk in "white garments" without any defilement, that their name would not be erased out of the book of life but confessed by the Lord before His Father and His Father's angels (3:1-2, 4-5).

H. The overcomers keep the Lord's word of endurance and do not deny the Lord's name unto the last bit of their power, that they may be kept out of the hour of trial, which is coming to try all those who dwell on the earth, and that they may receive the crown of reward to be pillars in the temple of God with the name of God, the name of the city of God, the New Jerusalem, and Christ's new name written upon them (vv. 8b, 10-12).

I. The overcomers are hot, instead of being lukewarm, to buy gold refined by fire, white garments, and eyesalve so that they may not be spewed out of the Lord's mouth but may be invited to dine with the Lord and to sit with Him on His throne (vv. 15-21).

Day 5

IV. **The overcomers enjoy the sevenfold intensified Spirit to become the testimony of Jesus (1:2, 9; 19:10):**

A. The testimony of Jesus is the seven golden lampstands as the shining churches—divine in nature, shining in darkness, and identical with one another (1:11-20).

B. The testimony of Jesus is the great multitude serving God in the heavenly temple, the whole Body of God's redeemed, who have been raptured to the heavens to enjoy God's care and the Lamb's shepherding (7:9-17).

C. The testimony of Jesus is the bright woman, representing the whole Body of God's redeemed, with her man-child, representing the overcomers as the stronger part of God's people (12:1-17).

Day 6 D. The testimony of Jesus is the firstfruits, signifying the overcomers raptured before the great tribulation, and the harvest, signifying the majority of the believers raptured at the end of the great tribulation (14:1-5, 14-16).

E. The testimony of Jesus is the victorious ones standing on the glassy sea, signifying the late overcomers who will pass through the great tribulation and overcome Antichrist and the worshipping of Antichrist (15:2-4).

F. The testimony of Jesus is the bride ready for marriage, consisting of the overcoming saints during the millennium (19:7-9).

G. The testimony of Jesus is the bridal army to fight in oneness with Christ, the embodiment of God, and to defeat Antichrist, the embodiment of Satan, with his armies (vv. 14-19; 17:14).

H. Ultimately, the testimony of Jesus is the New Jerusalem, the great universal, divine-human incorporation of the processed and consummated Triune God with His regenerated, transformed, and glorified tripartite people (21:2-3, 22; cf. Exo. 38:21) and the unique lampstand as the consummation of all the lampstands for the consummate expression of God (Rev. 21:18, 23; 22:5).

Morning Nourishment

Rev.   John to the seven churches which are in Asia: Grace
1:4   to you and peace from Him who is and who was and
       who is coming, and from the seven Spirits who are
       before His throne.
Psa.   When I considered this in order to understand *it,* it
73:16-17   was a troublesome task in my sight, until I went into
       the sanctuary of God; *then* I perceived their end.

The seven lamps...are a crucial item of the golden lampstand.
The main emphasis of the golden lampstand is its shining, and
the shining depends on the seven lamps.

In the universe, God has a center of administration, which is His
throne. Revelation 4:5 says that lightnings and voices and thunders come forth out of the throne. Lightnings, voices, and thunders
are signs, symbols, signifying that God is administering and moving from His throne to execute His eternal policy....Verse 5 also
says that "the seven Spirits of God" are "seven lamps of fire burning before the throne."...The seven lamps on the golden lampstand
are the seven lamps of fire before the throne of God. This signifies
that the seven lamps are absolutely related to God's administration, economy, and move. God's move depends on these seven
lamps. (*The Ultimate Significance of the Golden Lampstand,* p. 44)

Today's Reading

The lampstand was placed in the tabernacle, and in the tabernacle there was no door or window....Therefore, in the tabernacle
it was dark, having neither sunlight nor moonlight. However, in
the Holy Place there was a golden lampstand, which had...seven
lamps shining and illumining.

Both the sunlight and the moonlight are natural light for us to
observe natural things....However, natural light cannot help us
to know God's administration, God's economy, and God's eternal
purpose. To know God's administration and economy, we must
have the light of the golden lampstand. When we enter into the
realm of God's presence, there is no light without the golden
lampstand. Outside of the realm of God's presence, we have

sunlight and moonlight, and we have the natural view, but we can never have the view of God's economy and administration.

The light of the golden lampstand is the light of God's administration. Even though the tabernacle is small, the mercy seat, [or expiation cover,] within it is the throne of God. God's throne is in the tabernacle, and before the throne are the seven bright burning lamps. When we enter into the tabernacle, we cannot do anything without these seven bright lamps, because without them, we are not able to see anything. When a priest entered into the tabernacle, his actions were dependent upon the shining of these seven bright lamps. The light of the seven bright lamps dictated all the actions of the priests in the tabernacle. This is the way of God's administration, government, and economy.

The light of the golden lampstand is the light of the Holy Place. ...The Holy Place today is the church. The church is the lampstand, and it is also the Holy Place....When we come to the church meetings,...as soon as we are seated, we are enlightened! We are clear!...As long as we come into the realm of the church, all we have to do is sit in the meetings, and meeting after meeting we will become clear inwardly. We will receive a thorough understanding of human life, and we will become completely clear about God's will. We will be crystal clear about God's economy, and we will know the age which we are in today. This is due to the light in the Holy Place.

Once we go into the Holy Place, we understand [Psa. 73:16-17]. This is because in the Holy Place is the throne, the One who sits on the throne, and the presence of God, and before the throne of God is the shining of the seven burning lamps of fire. Once we enter into this realm, immediately we are clear. We know God's eternal purpose, His heart's intention, and His economy, and we also know which path we should take for the journey before us. This is due to the light in the Holy Place. (*The Ultimate Significance of the Golden Lampstand,* pp. 45-46, 48-50)

Further Reading: The Ultimate Significance of the Golden Lampstand, ch. 4

Enlightenment and inspiration: _____

_____

_____

_____

Morning Nourishment

Rev. ...And *there were* seven lamps of fire burning before
4:5 the throne, which are the seven Spirits of God.
5:6 And I saw in the midst of the throne...a Lamb
      standing as having *just* been slain, having seven
      horns and seven eyes, which are the seven Spirits of
      God sent forth into all the earth.

Sometimes, in certain local churches...there is only a small
amount of light. In 1 Samuel 3, when Samuel ministered to Jehovah as a child before Eli, "the lamp of God had not yet gone out"
(v. 3). This means that the lamp was about to go out because old
Eli the priest was too weak. Exodus says that the lamps in the
Holy Place were lit by the priests. The priests had to burn the
incense when they dressed the lamps in the morning and when
they lit them in the evening. To burn the incense is to pray.
Whether or not the lamps of a local church are bright is absolutely
related to the priests' burning of incense before God. The reason
that the lamps are not bright is that the service, the priesthood,
and the burning of incense are absent. Although the Holy Place
and the lampstand are real, the priestly ministry may be weak,
like that of Eli....Whether or not the light of the lamps is bright is
absolutely related to the service of the priesthood.

Each one of us has a share in the priesthood,...and we all have
to learn to fulfill our duty of burning the incense,...pray[ing] at
night and in the morning so that the light of God may shine
brightly among us. The light should be so bright that the illumining of the light becomes God's move, His administration, His government in the universe, and His economy on earth today. (*The
Ultimate Significance of the Golden Lampstand,* pp. 50-52)

Today's Reading

After the seven lamps of fire [Rev. 4:5] burn in us, they become
seven eyes [5:6]. It is wonderful that the shining lamps become
the lamps of fire, and the lamps of fire become the eyes....A person's loveliness is in his eyes. Thank the Lord that the shining
and burning lamps eventually become the lovely eyes....These

seven lamps are the seven eyes of God.

Eyes are not only for seeing but also for transfusing. What does transfusing mean? It is to transmit a person's inner being into the one he is looking at….To transfuse is to infuse. Whether the transfusion is of love or of fear, God has been transfused into us.

The church is the place where God transfuses….Every time we meet together, we allow God to transfuse Himself into us. This is the reality of the church….When we come to the church meetings, we feel that we are sitting before the Lord and that His eyes are looking at us. If we obey Him, we feel that He is lovely. If we disobey Him, He is still lovely, but we are a little ashamed. We may say, "O Lord, in the past week I disobeyed You. Lord, forgive me and wash me with Your precious blood."…This is the transfusion and infusion of the Lord's inner being into us for our transformation. Transformation is not a change caused by a shining light; rather, it is the transfusing of the Lord's lovable person into us…. This transfusion goes on week by week until…there is something wonderful in us and…we have had a great change. Such an experience is the reality of the church.

The seven eyes are in the church….The seven eyes are on the lampstand, and the lampstand is in the Holy Place….To receive the transfusion of the seven eyes we must be in the church.

Second Chronicles 16:9 says, "The eyes of Jehovah run to and fro throughout all the earth." Today God's eyes are running to and fro, seeking those whose heart is perfect towards Him. Psalm 32:8 says, "I will instruct you and teach you concerning the way you should go; / I will counsel you; my eye is upon you." The Lord guides us not mainly with words or other indications but with His eyes. The guiding of the eyes is the most intimate kind, and it is used between those who are intimate. When two very intimate people speak with one another,…they may use [only] their eyes. (*The Ultimate Significance of the Golden Lampstand,* pp. 67-69, 71)

Further Reading: The Ultimate Significance of the Golden Lampstand, ch. 5

Enlightenment and inspiration: _____

_____

_____

_____

Morning Nourishment

Rev. But I have *one thing* against you, that you have left
2:4-5 your first love. Remember therefore where you have
       fallen from and repent and do the first works...
   7 ...To him who overcomes, to him I will give to eat of
       the tree of life, which is in the Paradise of God.

Revelation 2 and 3 reveal that we need to [be the overcomers who] conquer all the satanic chaos and carry out the unique divine economy in certain conditions.

We need to be those who love the Lord with the first love (Rev. 2:4). The first love may be compared to the love of newlyweds. After a couple has been married for a period of time, it is easy for the first love to fade away. What wife loves her husband now as much as she did on her wedding day? We must recover the wedding, bridal love toward our Husband, Christ.

We also need to enjoy eating Christ as the tree of life in the church as today's Paradise so that we can be a shining lampstand (vv. 7, 5). The Lord...tells the overcomers that He will give them to eat of the...tree of life, which is Christ Himself. We should eat...the tree of life, which is Christ as the embodiment of the divine life.

We have to love the Lord with a bridal love, and we have to enjoy Him as the...tree of life. This tree is growing in the Paradise of God. The Paradise of God (v. 7) is the New Jerusalem in the millennial kingdom,...[but] today the church life is the precursor of this coming paradise, the miniature of the New Jerusalem in the coming kingdom. (*The Satanic Chaos in the Old Creation and the Divine Economy for the New Creation*, p. 77)

Today's Reading

The Lord exhorted the church in Smyrna to be faithful unto death in suffering poverty and trial for the crown of life (Rev. 2:9-10). A crown in New Testament usage always denotes a prize that is in addition to salvation.

We have to enjoy Christ as the hidden manna, a special portion of the nourishing supply, to overcome the worldliness of the degraded church with the idolatrous teaching of Balaam and the hierarchical teaching of the Nicolaitans (Rev. 2:12-17a). The Lord gave manna to the children of Israel openly…(Exo. 16:14-18). But a small portion of this manna was preserved in a golden pot within the Ark in the tabernacle (16:33; Heb. 9:4). That is the hidden manna. The open manna is Christ as the common portion to all of God's people for them to enjoy in a public way. The hidden manna, signifying the hidden Christ, is a special portion reserved for His overcoming seekers, who overcome the degradation of the worldly church.

Only the overcoming seekers who enter into the Holy of Holies to experience Christ as the Ark, God's testimony, enjoy a particular portion of the hidden Christ. We must have some deeper experience of Christ. Our experience of Christ should not merely be openly in the meetings, but hiddenly in the Holy of Holies, even in Christ Himself as the Ark, the testimony of God. In Christ as the Ark, we can enjoy Him as the hidden manna, as a particular portion for our life supply, to overcome the worldliness of the degraded church.

Such a worldly church has the idolatrous teaching of Balaam and the hierarchical teaching of the Nicolaitans. Today in Christendom these two kinds of teachings are prevailing.…The teaching of Balaam distracts believers from the person of Christ to idolatry and from the enjoyment of Christ to spiritual fornication, [and] the teaching of the Nicolaitans builds up a hierarchy among the believers,…destroy[ing] the function of believers as members of the Body of Christ, thus annulling the Lord's Body as His expression.

In the Lord's recovery,…all of us have the position as members of the Body of Christ to speak for the Lord…and teach the truth. Our speaking for the Lord in the meetings is the annulling of the hierarchy.…The Lord desires to recover the functioning of all the members of the Body of Christ. (*The Satanic Chaos in the Old Creation and the Divine Economy for the New Creation,* pp. 78-79)

Further Reading: The Satanic Chaos in the Old Creation and the Divine Economy for the New Creation, ch. 3; *The Overcomers,* ch. 1; *Elders' Training, Book 5: Fellowship concerning the Lord's Up-to-date Move,* ch. 2

Enlightenment and inspiration: _____

_____
_____
_____

Morning Nourishment

Rev. ...To him who overcomes, to him I will give of the
2:17 hidden manna, and to him I will give a white stone,
and upon the stone a new name written, which no
one knows except him who receives *it.*

3:5 He who overcomes will be clothed thus, in white garments, and I shall by no means erase his name out of
the book of life, and I will confess his name before
My Father and before His angels.

God's work of building the church depends upon our transformation. As the overcomers, we need to be transformed to be a "white
stone," justified and approved by the Lord, for the building up of the
house of God, with a "new name" according to the transformation
in life (Rev. 2:17b). In our natural being, we are not stones but clay.
But we are being transformed from clay into precious stones for
God's building. The color white signifies justification and approval.
When we are transformed into a white stone, this means that we
are justified and approved by the Lord for His building.

Some houses are made of adobe, but not the church. The
church is built up with precious stones. These precious stones are
the believers who have experienced transformation upon transformation (Rom. 12:2; 2 Cor. 3:18). Every transformed believer, as
a white stone, bears a new name. Such a new name is the inter-
pretation of the experience of the one who has been transformed.
Hence, only he himself knows the meaning of that name. We
receive a new name by our new experience according to the transformation in life. (*The Satanic Chaos in the Old Creation and the
Divine Economy for the New Creation,* pp. 79-80)

Today's Reading

We need to be those who stand strongly against the Romish
teaching of Jezebel, which is full of fornication, idolatry, and the
deep things of Satan (Rev. 2:20, 24a). The Romish teaching of
Jezebel is the teaching of the apostate Roman Catholic Church.
This is clearly seen in the church in Thyatira in Revelation 2.

We have pointed out that with the church in Sardis in

Revelation 3, everything is either dead or dying. In order to be the overcomers, we need to flee spiritual death. We need to be those who live in reality with nothing dying in imperfection. As the overcomers, we should walk in "white garments" without any defilement, so that our name will not be erased out of the book of life but confessed by the Lord before His Father and His Father's angels in the next age—the kingdom age (Rev. 3:1-2, 4-5). To walk in white garments is to have a living that is unspotted by death and that is justified and approved in life by the Lord.

The overcomers in Philadelphia keep the Lord's word of endurance and do not deny the Lord's name unto the last bit of their power, that they may be kept out of the hour of trial which is coming to try all those who dwell on the earth and that they may receive the crown of reward to be pillars in the temple of God with the name of God, the name of the city of God, the New Jerusalem, and Christ's new name written upon them (Rev. 3:8b, 10-12). The hour of trial will be the time of the great tribulation. For all of these points concerning the overcomers it would be helpful to study Revelation 2 and 3 with all the notes in the Recovery Version. Then we will be able to understand much more.

We need to be hot, even burning, instead of being lukewarm, to buy gold refined by fire, white garments, and eyesalve, that we may not be spewed out of the Lord's mouth, but may be invited to dine with the Lord and to sit with Him on His throne (Rev. 3:15-21). We need to be those who dine, who feast, with the Lord in this age so that we can sit on the throne with the Lord in the kingdom age. To sit with the Lord on His throne will be a prize to the overcomer, that he may participate in the Lord's authority and be a co-king with Him to rule over the whole earth in the coming millennial kingdom. (*The Satanic Chaos in the Old Creation and the Divine Economy for the New Creation,* pp. 80-81)

Further Reading: The Satanic Chaos in the Old Creation and the Divine Economy for the New Creation, ch. 3; *The Testimony of Jesus,* ch. 10

Enlightenment and inspiration: _____

_____

_____

_____

Morning Nourishment

Rev. Saying, What you see write in a scroll and send *it* to
1:11-12 the seven churches: to Ephesus and to Smyrna and
to Pergamos and to Thyatira and to Sardis and to
Philadelphia and to Laodicea. And I turned to see the
voice that spoke with me; and when I turned, I saw
seven golden lampstands.

As the local churches, the lampstands are golden in nature. In
typology, gold signifies divinity, the divine nature of God. All the
local churches are divine in nature; they are constituted with the
divine nature of God....This means that...without divinity, there
can be no church. Although the church is composed of humanity
with divinity, humanity should not be the basic nature of the local
churches. The basic nature of the local churches must be divinity,
God's divine nature.

The lampstands shine in the darkness....For the lamp to shine, it
must have oil burning within it. If the oil burns within the lamp, the
light will shine out through all the darkness. This is the function of
the church. The function of the church is not simply to preach or to
teach doctrine. In the dark night of this age, the church must shine
out the very glory of God. This is the testimony of the church.

All the lampstands are identical....All the differences in the
local churches in Revelation 2 and 3 are negative, not positive.
Ephesus lost her first love—negative; Pergamos is worldly—negative; Thyatira is demonic—negative; and Laodicea became
lukewarm—negative. On the positive side, however, all the local
churches are identical, because they all are seven golden lampstands. If you could place all the seven lampstands on a table
before you, unless you numbered or labeled them, you would be
unable to tell them apart. All the seven lampstands are the same.
(*Life-study of Revelation,* pp. 28-29)

Today's Reading

In Revelation 7:9-17 we see the testimony of Jesus as the great
multitude....This great multitude is the whole Body of God's
redeemed ones, having been redeemed "out of every nation and

all tribes and peoples and tongues" (7:9)....This great multitude has come out of tribulation [v. 14] in a victorious way, for they all hold palm branches which signify their victory over tribulation (v. 9). Eventually, in eternity, they will be overshadowed by God with His tabernacle [v. 15]....Furthermore, they will also be shepherded by the Lamb at the springs of waters of life for eternity (v. 17)....All God's redeemed ones eventually will be raptured to the throne of God and will stand there enjoying God's overshadowing and the Lamb's shepherding.

In 12:1-17 we see another symbol of the church: the woman with the man-child....The woman in this chapter represents the whole Body of God's people, and the man-child represents the stronger part of God's people. As there is the man-child within the woman, so among God's people there is a stronger part. This woman, who is bright with the sun, the moon, and twelve stars (12:1) and who is persecuted by Satan, the great red dragon, represents God's people throughout all the generations. In every generation, a portion of God's people has always been persecuted by Satan.

The woman will be left on earth to pass through the tribulation, but the stronger part, the man-child, will be raptured to the throne of God before the tribulation. Why will the man-child be raptured prior to the tribulation? Because God needs the man-child to fight Satan in the heavens and to cast him down....The man-child will fight through and up, fighting up to the throne to cast Satan down from the heavens to the earth. This is a part of the testimony of Jesus. Although Jesus has defeated Satan on the cross, there is still the need for the church to execute His victory over the enemy. Because so many members of the Body have failed in this matter, only the stronger part of the Body, the man-child, will execute Christ's victory over Satan. The man-child will be raptured to the heavens to accomplish this job. (*Life-study of Revelation,* pp. 30-32)

Further Reading: The Testimony of Jesus, ch. 9; *Life-study of Revelation,* msg. 3

Enlightenment and inspiration: _____

_____

_____

_____

Morning Nourishment

Rev. And I saw...the Lamb standing on Mount Zion, and
14:1 with Him a hundred and forty-four thousand...
    4 ...These are they who follow the Lamb wherever
       He may go. These were purchased from among
       men *as* firstfruits to God and to the Lamb.
   15 And another angel came out of the temple, crying
       with a loud voice to Him who sat on the cloud, Send
       forth Your sickle and reap, for the hour to reap has
       come because the harvest of the earth is ripe.

Now we come to the firstfruits and the harvest (Rev. 14:1-5,
14-16). The church is...a field growing a crop which must ripen
and become mature. Any crop which is still green is too tender to
be harvested. But once the crop has ripened in the field, it will be
harvested immediately.

That part of the crop which ripens first is called the firstfruits.
The firstfruits will be raptured to Zion in the heavens before the
great tribulation....The firstfruits are those who "follow the Lamb
wherever He may go" [v. 4]....The firstfruits...are raptured to the
house of God in Zion as the fresh enjoyment to God. This is for
God's satisfaction....In the Old Testament, the firstfruits of the ripened harvest were taken not to the barn but into the temple of God
(Exo. 23:19). This indicates that all the early overcomers will be
taken up to the house of God in heaven for God's enjoyment. The
rapture is not mainly for our enjoyment but for God's enjoyment.
The rapture is for defeating the enemy and for satisfying God.

The harvest [Rev. 14:14-16] will be reaped near the end of the
great tribulation. It will be raptured to the air where Christ will
be on the cloud....The great tribulation will be the strong sun-
shine, which will ripen all the saints who will not be ready before
the tribulation. To put it simply, if today you do not give up the
world and live for Christ, Christ will leave you on earth to pass
through the great tribulation. At that time, you will surely give up
the world and realize that the best way to live is to live for Christ.
All the children of God must do this; otherwise, they could never
ripen. (*Life-study of Revelation*, pp. 32-34)

Today's Reading

In Revelation 15:2-4 we see the overcomers…[who] will pass through the great tribulation…[and] overcome the beast, his image, and the worship of the idol of the Antichrist. Revelation 20:4 and 6 indicate that some of the co-kings of Christ will be these late overcomers.…If you are sloppy, you will be left to pass through the great tribulation. We all must look to the Lord and say, "Lord, I want to be an early overcomer."

In 19:7-9 we see the church as the bride.…The bride will wear bright raiment, being clothed with bright and pure righteousness, and will be invited to the marriage feast of the Lamb (vv. 7-9). This is a very intimate matter. To God's enemy, we must be the man-child; for God's satisfaction, we must be the firstfruits; and for Christ, we must be the bride.

The church is also the army (vv. 14-19; 17:14). The part of the church which will be the man-child to fight against the enemy in the heavens will also be the army to fight with Christ against Satan on earth. After all the raptures have been completed and after the believers have been judged at the judgment seat of Christ, all the overcomers will come back to the earth with Christ as His army to fight against the Antichrist and his army.…Eventually, at the end of this war, Christ will defeat the Antichrist.

Ultimately, the testimony of Jesus will be the New Jerusalem (21:1—22:5). Beginning with the lampstand and passing through the great multitude, the man-child, the firstfruits, the late overcomers, the bride, and the army, all the saved ones will eventually be the New Jerusalem, which will be a living composition of all of God's redeemed ones, the ultimate consummation of God's building of His people. In and for eternity, the New Jerusalem will express God in the Lamb with the flow of the Spirit. (*Life-study of Revelation,* pp. 34-36)

Further Reading: Life-study of Revelation, msg. 3; *The Testimony of Jesus,* ch. 11

Enlightenment and inspiration: _____
_____
_____
_____

Hymns, #1259

1   See the local churches,
    'Midst the earth's dark night;
    Jesus' testimony,
    Bearing Him as light.
    Formed by Him, unmeasured,
    In the Spirit's mold—
    All are one in nature,
    One pure work of gold.

      See the local churches,
      'Midst the earth's dark night;
      Burning in the Spirit,
      Shining forth with Christ.

2   God in Christ, embodied,
    As God's lampstand, He
    Has become the Spirit,
    The reality.
    Spirit as the lampstand
    Has been multiplied;
    Many local churches,
    Now are realized!

3   Caring for the churches
    Is the Son of Man:
    Voice of many waters,
    Stars in His right hand;
    Eyes aflame; His face is
    Shining as the sun;
    Churches—fear no trial,
    He's the living One!

4   What can quench the lampstands?
    Who can them defy?
    More the opposition—
    More they multiply!
    Deeper darkness 'round them,
    Brighter do they shine.
    They are constituted
    With the life divine.

5   Soon the local churches
    Shall the Bride become,
    Bringing in that city—
    New Jerusalem.

Then the many lampstands
Shall one lampstand be;
Triune God expressing,
Universally.

   Lo, from heav'n descending,
   All the earth shall see
   God's complete expression,
   For eternity.

Composition for prophecy with main point and sub-points: _____

_____

_____

_____

_____

_____

_____

_____

_____

_____

_____

_____

_____

_____

_____

_____

_____

_____

_____

_____

_____

_____

_____

_____

_____

_____

_____

_____

_____

_____

_____

_____

Working with Christ
in the Stage of Intensification
to Bring Forth Golden Lampstands
Consummating in the New Jerusalem
as the Universal Golden Lampstand

Scripture Reading: Rev. 1:12, 20; 2:1; 4:5; 21:10, 18b, 23-24; 22:1, 5

Day 1   I. The New Testament economy consummates in the golden lampstands and in the New Jerusalem (Rev. 1:12, 20; 21:2, 10-11, 16, 18b, 23).

II. Christ carries out His mission as the Ruler of the kings of the earth by the seven burning Spirits before the throne to rule over the world situation so that the environment might be fit for God's chosen people to receive His salvation (Acts 5:31; 17:26-27; John 17:2; 2 Chron. 16:9).

III. The seven Spirits as the seven lamps of fire burning before the throne of God do not burn without a goal; there is a purpose for the burning of the seven Spirits—to bring forth the golden lampstands, the churches, for the fulfillment of God's New Testament economy (Rev. 4:5; 1:12, 20; 2:1):

Day 2   A. The sevenfold intensified Spirit is the seven lamps of fire before God's administrative throne to direct the world situation in order to execute God's economy in the universe (4:5):

   1. The seven Spirits of God are burning not only concerning the churches but also concerning the world situation for the churches; the flaming Spirits direct the world situation and also purify the churches to produce the golden lampstands (1:11-12).

   2. God will touch the earth by the seven lamps, by His seven Spirits, which are burning, shining, judging, purifying, refining, and

producing; the entire world situation is under the flame of the burning of the seven Spirits (4:5).

3. The seven Spirits are burning to judge, purify, and refine for the carrying out of God's economy to bring forth golden lampstands (1:20).

B. The burning of the seven Spirits as seven lamps of fire motivates us to rise up and take action for the carrying out of God's economy (Dan. 11:32b):

1. Our cooperation with God to complete His move depends upon our being intensified for His move (Rev. 3:1; 4:5; 5:6).

2. We all need to pray, "Dear divine Flame, come! Come and judge! Come and purify! Come and refine that You may produce the golden lampstand" (*God's New Testament Economy,* p. 241).

Day 3　IV. **The churches as golden lampstands will consummate in the New Jerusalem as the universal golden lampstand, the aggregate of all the lampstands (Rev. 1:20; 21:18b, 23):**

A. The New Jerusalem is the ultimate consummation of the lampstands in the Scriptures (Exo. 25:31-37; 1 Kings 7:49; Zech. 4:2; Rev. 1:12, 20).

B. In the book of Revelation there are two great signs—the sign of the golden lampstands and the sign of the New Jerusalem (vv. 1, 12, 20; 21:2, 10-11).

C. Revelation begins with the lampstands and ends with the lampstand (1:20; 21:18b, 23):

1. At the beginning of Revelation there are seven lampstands, the local lampstands in this age (2:1).

2. At the end of Revelation there is an aggregate, a composite, lampstand, the universal lampstand in eternity (21:18b, 23).

D. The New Jerusalem, a mountain of gold, is the universal golden lampstand holding the Lamb as the lamp shining out God as the light (vv. 18b, 23; 22:1, 5):

1. The New Jerusalem is a mountain of gold (21:18b, 21b; 22:1):

   a. If we consider the facts that the New Jerusalem is a golden city, that it has one street which reaches all twelve gates, and that it is twelve thousand stadia high, we will realize that the city proper is a golden mountain.

   b. As a golden mountain, the New Jerusalem is the ultimate, unique, and eternal golden lampstand absolutely composed of God's nature (gold).

Day 4

2. God as the light is in the Lamb as the lamp shining out from the top of the New Jerusalem as the universal golden lampstand (21:23; 22:1, 5):

   a. On the top of the golden mountain is the throne as the center, and on the throne is Christ the Lamb as the lamp with God in Him as the light shining out through the city (21:23; 22:5).

   b. The golden mountain is a stand, and upon this stand is a lamp; therefore, the golden mountain is a golden lampstand.

E. The New Jerusalem, the aggregate of all the lampstands, the totality of today's lampstands, is a consummate, universal golden lampstand to shine forth God's glory in the new heaven and new earth for eternity (21:24).

F. We become the New Jerusalem as the universal golden lampstand by becoming a golden mountain (vv. 16, 18b, 21b; 22:1):

1. In the Bible a mountain signifies resurrection and ascension; thus, we become a mountain by experiencing Christ in His resurrection and ascension (Eph. 2:5-6).

2. As a golden mountain, the New Jerusalem

comes out of the divine nature; thus, we become the New Jerusalem by partaking of the divine nature (2 Pet. 1:4).

3. The entire golden city is transparent; thus, we become a transparent mountain of gold by becoming transparent in the divine life and nature (Rev. 21:18b, 21b; 22:1).

*Day 5
&
Day 6*

4. As a golden mountain, the New Jerusalem is the unique, ultimate, and eternal golden lampstand, the aggregate of all the lampstands; thus, we become the New Jerusalem by living in and being a part of the church as a golden lampstand (21:23; 1:12, 20).

G. The golden lampstand signifies the Triune God embodied and expressed, and the more we experience the aspects of the Triune God depicted in the lampstand—the gold, the solid form, and the seven lamps—the more we will be in reality the golden lampstand as the embodiment and expression of the Triune God and thus become the New Jerusalem as the universal golden lampstand (Exo. 25:31, 36-37; Rev. 1:12, 20; 21:18b).

Morning Nourishment

Rev. The mystery of the seven stars which you saw upon
1:20 My right hand and the seven golden lampstands: The
seven stars are the messengers of the seven churches,
and the seven lampstands are the seven churches.
21:2 And I saw the holy city, New Jerusalem, coming down
out of heaven from God, prepared as a bride adorned
for her husband.
Acts This One God has exalted to His right hand as Leader
5:31 and Savior, to give repentance to Israel and forgiveness of sins.

According to...Revelation, the overcoming church consummates
in the golden lampstands and, ultimately, in the New Jerusalem.
The seven lampstands are in this age, and the New Jerusalem
will be in eternity. Therefore, the book of Revelation opens with
the seven lampstands and closes with the New Jerusalem.

In the first section of the New Testament [Matt.—John] we
have the initiation of God's New Testament economy, in the second
section [Acts—Jude] we have its development, and in the third
section [Rev.] we have its finalization. This means that the seven
Spirits as the intensification of the Triune God in the overcoming
church are the finalization of the New Testament economy...in
two stages: first, in this age, with the golden lampstands; finally,
in eternity, in the New Jerusalem. (*Life-study of Mark*, p. 590)

Today's Reading

The book of Revelation presents us a view of God's universal
administration....John was in his spirit and he saw a view in the
heavens concerning the earth. The heavens were opened to him
and he saw that there is a throne in the heavens. This throne is
the throne of God for His administration and is the center of God's
universal administration.

The seven Spirits of God burning before God's throne as a
flame of fire are judging the entire world, both the believers and
the unbelievers. According to 1 Peter 4:17 this judgment begins
from the house of God and will spread to the unbelievers, the

entire earth. The seven Spirits are sent forth unto all the earth to judge the earth, to purify the earth, to refine the earth, and to bring forth the pure golden lampstands, shining in this dark age as the testimony of Jesus....If we are shortsighted and do not have the foresight, we will be very much disappointed by today's world situation. Today's world is full of darkness, corruption, and immorality. Thank the Lord, however, that His Word is like a lamp shining in a dark place (2 Pet. 1:19), and His Word is as a lamp unto our feet and a light unto our path (Psa. 119:105). Because we have the foresight, we would not be disappointed. Many Christians and all the people of the world do not know what is going on behind the scenes in today's world situation. We realize, however,...that the seven Spirits today are burning to judge, to purify, and to refine with a purpose...to bring forth the golden lampstands, the churches, for the fulfillment of God's New Testament economy. (*God's New Testament Economy,* pp. 236-238)

In His work in the divine administration Christ is the Ruler of the kings of the earth [Rev. 1:5]. As the Ruler of the kings of the earth, Christ rules the whole earth that the gospel may be spread and the church may be produced. Apparently the earth is ruled by kings and presidents. Actually the earth is ruled by Christ, the highest Ruler, who is above all kings and presidents. If we study history in the light of the Bible, we shall realize that history has been altogether under the hand of Christ as the Ruler of the kings. He is ruling sovereignly over the earth with His authority so that the environment may be fit for God's chosen people to receive His salvation (Acts 17:26-27; John 17:2). He is managing the world's situation for the purpose of producing the church so that He may come back to establish the kingdom of God on earth. Now we need to do our part by being faithful to Him so that He may use us to spread the gospel and build up the church. (*The Conclusion of the New Testament,* p. 829)

Further Reading: The Divine Economy, ch. 14; *The Conclusion of the New Testament,* msg. 77

Enlightenment and inspiration: _____

_____
_____
_____

Morning Nourishment

Rev. ...What you see write in a scroll and send *it* to the
1:11　seven churches: to Ephesus and to Smyrna and to
Pergamos and to Thyatira and to Sardis and to Philadelphia and to Laodicea.
4:5　And out of the throne come forth lightnings and
voices and thunders. And *there were* seven lamps of
fire burning before the throne, which are the seven
Spirits of God.
Dan. ...The people who know their God will show
11:32　strength and take action.

The seven Spirits are burning on this earth today for the carrying out of God's administration. Christ carries out His mission
as the Ruler of the kings of the earth by the seven burning Spirits....Today the seven Spirits of God are burning not only concerning the churches but also concerning the world situation for the
churches. The entire world situation is under the flame of the
burning of the seven Spirits,...carrying out God's administration
on this earth. The world situation, the international affairs, are all
under the direction of this flame. I have seen the flame of the seven
burning Spirits before the throne of God sovereignly controlling
the world situation. (*God's New Testament Economy,* pp. 240-241)

Today's Reading

The purpose of the burning flame in carrying out God's economy is to bring forth the golden lampstands, the churches. Burning implies judging, purifying, refining, and producing. Never be
disappointed by the rottenness, corruption, and immorality of
today's human society. Do not be disappointed or so concerned for
the world situation. Also, do not be disappointed by the weakness
of the local churches. I do not believe in the seemingly disappoint-
ing condition in the world or in the churches. I believe in the flame
of the burning seven Spirits which control and direct the world
and which also judge, purify, and refine the church to produce a
pure golden lampstand. We are here endeavoring to afford the
Lord a chance and an entrance to judge us, purify us, and refine

us to produce a pure golden lampstand. We are open wide to the flaming of the seven Spirits of God. We all need to pray, "Dear divine Flame, come! Come and judge! Come and purify! Come and refine that You may produce the golden lampstand." Nearly all the doors are closed to Christ in today's situation. By His mercy, though, we are open to Him. ...I do not know how much you pray or how you pray, but I can testify that nearly every day I pray, "Lord, enlighten me; search me within and expose me, Lord. I like to be enlightened by You and exposed in Your light." Are you like this or do you shut yourself up and hide something from Him? We all need to pray, "Lord, we are open. Come and shine upon us and shine from within us and enlighten every avenue and every corner of our being. I like to be exposed, purged, and purified." Then the Lord has a way to produce a pure golden lampstand. The burning is going on not only in the entire world situation, but also in the churches.

The seven Spirits, who are out from the eternal One and of the redeeming One, are the seven lamps of fire burning before God's throne, executing God's economy in the universe, and the seven eyes of the slain Lamb, searching and infusing the churches (4:5; 5:6b). The twofold mission of the seven Spirits is to carry out God's administration and to search and infuse the churches....The seven Spirits of God as the eyes of the Lamb infuse us with this wonderful One's burden and essence. (*God's New Testament Economy*, pp. 241-242)

In the age of Revelation, the Spirit has been intensified sevenfold....In this dark age we need the sevenfold intensified Spirit. Many Christians appreciate what is recorded in the four Gospels and the Acts,...but they should appreciate even more what we have today. Today what we experience is the sevenfold intensified Spirit. In order to be the overcomers, we need such a Spirit. (*The Spirit with Our Spirit*, pp. 54-55)

Further Reading: God's New Testament Economy, ch. 23; *Life-study of Revelation*, msg. 8; *The Spirit with Our Spirit*, ch. 5

Enlightenment and inspiration: _____

_____

_____

_____

Morning Nourishment

Rev. And I turned to see the voice that spoke with
1:12 me; and when I turned, I saw seven golden lampstands.
21:18 And the building work of its wall was jasper;
and the city was pure gold, like clear glass.
23 And the city has no need of the sun or of the
moon that they should shine in it, for the glory of
God illumined it, and its lamp is the Lamb.

The churches as golden lampstands will be consummated
in the New Jerusalem. The New Jerusalem, the holy city, is
the aggregate of all the lampstands. If we consider the facts
that the New Jerusalem is a golden city (Rev. 21:18b), that it
has one street which reaches all twelve gates (Rev. 21:21;
22:2), that the wall of the city is one hundred forty-four cubits
high (21:17), and that the city itself is twelve thousand stadia
high (21:16), we shall realize that the city proper must be a
mountain. On top of this mountain is a throne, from which the
street spirals down to the bottom to reach the twelve gates.
On top of this golden mountain is the throne as the center. On
the throne is Christ as the Lamb with God in Him (22:1). This
Lamb is the lamp with God in Him as the light (21:23; 22:5).
(*The Conclusion of the New Testament,* p. 2345)

Today's Reading

In the book of Revelation, which is the conclusion of the
New Testament and even of the entire Bible, there are two
great signs. In chapter one there is the sign of the golden
lampstands, and in chapters twenty-one and twenty-two there
is the greatest sign, the sign of the New Jerusalem. The New
Jerusalem is the aggregate of all the lampstands. At the beginning of Revelation, there are seven lampstands, the local lampstands in this age. At the end of Revelation, there is an
aggregate, a composite lampstand, the universal lampstand
in eternity. Therefore, Revelation begins with the lampstands

and ends with the lampstand. The lampstands are signs of the churches, whereas the New Jerusalem is a sign of God's eternal dwelling place and of Christ's wife, His eternal counterpart.

The New Jerusalem, the holy city, is a mountain of gold (Rev. 21:18)....As a mountain of gold, the New Jerusalem is the ultimate, unique, and eternal golden lampstand. Upon this stand is a lamp—Christ with God in Him as the light shining out through eternity. The holy city as a mountain of gold is the aggregate of all the lampstands (1:20), the totality of today's lampstands, shining forth God's glory in eternity in the new heaven and the new earth.

The city proper, a mountain of gold, is of the divine substance, element, and nature. In typology gold signifies the divine nature. The city proper is composed absolutely of the divine nature, the nature of God. The New Jerusalem itself comes out of the divine nature.

As believers in Christ and children of God, we all are a part of the New Jerusalem as a mountain of gold. When we were regenerated, we received the nature of God, and now we are partakers of the divine nature (2 Pet. 1:4). This means that a part of the golden mountain has entered into our being. We all have a part of the golden mountain, the New Jerusalem, within us. We need to realize that something within us is divine. A part of our regenerated being is "gold," and this gold is the divine nature. If we see the vision of the New Jerusalem built with gold, with the divine nature, and if we realize that as the children of God partaking of the divine nature we have a part of the golden mountain, we will renounce everything that does not belong to the divine nature and reject anything that does not match it. (*The Conclusion of the New Testament,* pp. 2688, 2708-2709)

Further Reading: The Conclusion of the New Testament, msg. 259; *The Divine Economy,* ch. 15

Enlightenment and inspiration: _____

_____

_____

_____

Morning Nourishment

2 Pet. ...That through these you might become partakers of
1:4   the divine nature...

Rev. And night will be no more; and they have no need of
22:5 the light of a lamp and of the light of the sun, for the
      Lord God will shine upon them; and they will reign
      forever and ever.

21:24 And the nations will walk by its light...

This golden mountain is a stand, and upon this stand is a lamp. Therefore, this golden mountain—the New Jerusalem—is a golden lampstand. As a golden lampstand, it has Christ as the lamp with God in Him as the light shining out for eternity. Thus, the New Jerusalem, the aggregate of all the lampstands, the totality of today's lampstands, is a consummate, universal golden lampstand to shine forth God's glory in the new heaven and new earth for eternity. (*The Conclusion of the New Testament*, p. 2345)

Today's Reading

In the church age, the lamps are the seven Spirits, but when we arrive in the New Jerusalem, the lamp will be the Lamb....God is the light, and the Lamb is the lamp. This means that God is in Christ, shining out over the city. Today, God Himself through the Spirit is shining on the stands with all the churches. In eternity, the entire New Jerusalem will be a golden lampstand. If we read Revelation 21 and 22 properly, we see that the New Jerusalem is a mountain of gold, just like a golden stand. The throne of God and the Lamb is on the top. This is God in Christ shining out as the light. Christ is the lamp, and within this lamp is God as the light. Therefore, Christ shines out God, and the city shines out Christ. Then the whole earth will walk in the light of the city. (*The Wonderful Christ in the Canon of the New Testament*, p. 225)

"The city was pure gold, like clear glass" [Rev. 21:18b]. Since gold signifies the divine nature, the nature of God, the city being pure is altogether of the divine nature....The whole city is transparent and not in the least opaque....As a golden mountain, the New Jerusalem is the ultimate, unique, and eternal golden lampstand, absolutely composed of God's nature. If we see the vision of the New Jerusalem built with the nature of God, we shall renounce everything that does not belong to God's nature and reject anything that does not match it. (*The Conclusion of the New Testament,* p. 2346)

The expression of God the Father as the source of all the divine riches is based upon His nature typified by gold (Rev. 21:18b).... The city itself is a mountain of gold. [Hence], God's divine nature is the very base, ground, and site of the city. The triune expression of the Father is not only based upon His nature but also is in His glory (Rev. 21:11). The New Jerusalem does not need any natural or man-made light because God Himself is the light of the city. Light is the nature of God's expression. God Himself is signified as gold in His intrinsic nature, and God being light denotes His nature in His expression. When this light shines, this shining becomes His glory....The triune expression of the Father as the source of all the divine riches is based upon His golden nature in His shining glory.

This vision should be applied to us today in our practical life. Revelation tells us that the city itself is gold (21:18) and that the street of the city is pure gold as transparent glass (21:21). This means that the golden mountain in our experience becomes our way or our street. The divine gold which is pure and transparent should be our walkway in our daily life. The walkway in today's church life is God's pure and transparent divine nature. In the church life, you must be pure, transparent, frank, straight, and open; you must be divine....If you walk, behave, and have your being in God's divine nature as your walkway, God's light will shine from within you and this shining is His glory. When others come to your home, they will have the realization that glory is there. In your daily life, family life, business life, and church life, others should be able to see the divine gold, the divine shining glory. (*God's New Testament Economy,* pp. 447-448)

Further Reading: The Conclusion of the New Testament, msg. 220; *The Wonderful Christ in the Canon of the New Testament,* chs. 21, 23

Enlightenment and inspiration: _____
_____
_____

Morning Nourishment

Exo. And you shall make a lampstand of pure gold. The
25:31 lampstand *with* its base and its shaft shall be made
of beaten work; its cups, its calyxes, and its blossom
buds shall be of *one piece with* it.
36-37 Their calyxes and their branches shall be of *one piece*
with it; all of it one beaten work of pure gold. And
you shall make its lamps, seven; and set up its lamps
to give light to the area in front of it.

As the testimony of Jesus, the golden lampstands are the
embodiment of the Triune God. In the golden lampstand there
are three main factors: the substance, the shape or form, and the
expression. The substance, the material, of the lampstand is gold,
which signifies the Father's divine essence.

There was no dross in the lampstand, for it was made of
pure gold. In typology, dross signifies something other than God
brought in to cause a mixture. The fact that the church is a golden
lampstand indicates that we should not bring anything other
than God into the church life. Even good things such as ethics,
culture, education, and proper religion are dross, because they are
not God Himself. Only God, the Divine Being, is the gold which is
the substance of the lampstand. No doubt Paul had this realization when he told us in 1 Corinthians 3 that upon Christ, the
unique foundation of the church, we should build not with wood,
grass, or stubble but with gold, silver, and precious stones.

As the local churches, the lampstands are golden in nature. In
typology, gold signifies divinity, the divine nature of God. All the
local churches are divine in nature; they are constituted of
the divine essence. These stands are not built of clay, wood, or
any inferior substance; they are constructed out of pure gold.
This means that all the local churches must be divine. Without
divinity, there can be no church. Although the church is composed
of humanity with divinity, humanity should not be the basic
nature of the local churches. The basic nature of the local
churches must be divinity. (*The Conclusion of the New Testament,*
pp. 2342-2343)

Today's Reading

The golden lampstand is not a lump of gold but gold in a definite form and purposeful shape. The form, the shape, of the lampstand signifies the Son's human form. Christ, the Son, is the embodiment of the Godhead, the embodiment of the Father's nature (Col. 2:9). Therefore, the church should have not only the Father's divine essence but also the Son's human form.

The fact that the form of the lampstand signifies the Son as the embodiment of the Godhead indicates that the church should not be vague but should have a definite shape. In chapters two and three of Revelation the Lord Jesus, as the embodiment of the invisible God, was clearly standing as He spoke to the churches. All the churches should also stand, having the Son's shape.

Furthermore, the golden lampstands as the testimony of Jesus have the Spirit's expression. The seven lamps of the lampstand shine for God's expression. These seven lamps are the seven Spirits of God. Thus,…we can say that the golden lampstand signifies the embodiment of the Triune God, with the Father as the substance, the Son as the form, and the Spirit as the expression.

To say that the church is the embodiment of the Triune God is not to make the church a part of deity or an object of worship. We mean that the church is an entity born of God (John 1:12-13), possessing God's life (1 John 5:11-12) and enjoying God's nature (2 Pet. 1:4). The church has the divine substance, bears the likeness of Christ, and expresses God.

As…the golden lampstand, the church is the embodiment of the Triune God to express Him. As members of Christ, we are sons of God born of Him, having His life and possessing His nature. Now we are learning to live by this life and nature that we may be filled and saturated with the processed Triune God to become His corporate expression through the sevenfold, intensified Spirit. (*The Conclusion of the New Testament,* pp. 2343-2344)

Further Reading: Life-study of Exodus, msgs. 92-94

Enlightenment and inspiration: _____

_____

_____

_____

Morning Nourishment

Exo. [The lampstand] shall be made of a talent of pure
25:39 gold, with all these utensils.
John God is Spirit, and those who worship Him must wor-
4:24 ship in spirit and truthfulness.
20:22 And when He had said this, He breathed into *them*
and said to them, Receive the Holy Spirit.

In order to have a lampstand, there must be a talent of gold
(Exo. 25:39)....We need more gold, more of God. If we would have
the church as the lampstand, we must have something substan-
tial—the gold, which is the substance, the essence, the element, of
God Himself. If we do not have this substance, all our talk about
the church is vain....How we need God as the golden element!
(*Life-study of Revelation,* pp. 363-364)

Today's Reading

We must receive God Himself as the golden element into the
depths of our being....Never close yourself to Him or shut any
part of your being to Him. Rather, tell Him, "O God, I am absolutely open to You. I exercise my spirit to contact You, the divine
Spirit. O divine Spirit, come into me and saturate me." This is the
way to gain more gold.

If we all gain more gold,...we shall be exceedingly rich in the
divine element, in the material for the lampstand. All the brothers and sisters will be full of God, and...when we enter into the
saints' homes, we shall see nothing but gold.

However, it is not adequate merely to have a large quantity of
gold. We may have a thousand talents of gold and not yet have the
lampstand, for we may just have the substance without the form.
How can we have the form?...The lampstand was made by beat-
ing the gold....All the gold must be brought together into one.
This refers to the building....It is a shame to the Lord if today He
cannot see any building....You may even have a great deal of gold,
but if you do not have the form, by the way of the building, you do
not have the lampstand. This means that you may be rich in gold
but poor in the lampstand—the building.

If you would have the stand, you must be beaten together with others. You need to lose your identification. Do not say, "This is my gold. I'm spiritual." For you to be spiritual as an end in itself is meaningless as far as the lampstand is concerned. Your experience and enjoyment of God must be beaten together with that of others. Our gold must be put together, beaten, and built up as one entity, as one unit. Then we not only have the gold, but are also built into a golden lampstand. This is the church.

Even though we may have the gold and are beaten together and are built into one as a lampstand, we still need the seven lamps, the seven Spirits of God as the expression. If we do not have the seven Spirits of God, we shall be unable to shine to express God. Whether we are young or old, we daily need to be filled with the sevenfold Spirit of God. Whenever we are filled with God's sevenfold Spirit, we are living and shining. Because we are filled with the seven Spirits of God, we cannot be dead or dim. Being filled with the sevenfold divine *pneuma*,...nothing can suppress us.

When we are filled with the Spirit, we can function at any time. This function is not a performance—it is our living....When we all are filled with the sevenfold Spirit of God in the built-up church, this sevenfold Spirit of God will become the very expression of God in Christ. (*Life-study of Revelation,* pp. 364-367)

Eventually, the church should be the lampstand with God the Father's nature as the element, with God the Son's mold as a shape, and with God the Spirit's expression as the shining....This is the church life and this is what the Lord is after in His recovery today. God's New Testament economy, which is focused on one wonderful Person who has passed through all the processes, issues in this age in the golden lampstand to shine forth the testimony of Jesus. Eventually, in the coming eternity the issue will be the New Jerusalem and that issue will be much richer than the golden lampstand. (*God's New Testament Economy,* pp. 256-257)

Further Reading: Life-study of Revelation, msg. 31; *God's New Testament Economy,* ch. 44

Enlightenment and inspiration: _____
_____
_____
_____

Hymns, #1226

1   Oh, the church of Christ is glorious, and we are
        part of it—
      We're so happy that the Lord has made us one!
     There's a Body in the universe and we belong
        to it—
      Hallelujah, for the Lord has made us one!

          Hallelujah for the Body!
          We are members of the Body!
          We are wholly for the Body!
          Hallelujah, for the Lord has made us one!

2   Not the individual Christians, but a corporate
        entity—
      God must have it for His full expression now;
     Not just individual churches but the Body
        corporately—
      Hallelujah, we are in the Body now!

          Hallelujah for the Body!
          Satan trembles at the Body!
          We're victorious in the Body!
          Hallelujah, we are in the Body now!

3   There are seven golden lampstands in the nature
        all divine—
      Nothing natural does the Body life allow.
     When we're one and share God's nature, how
        the lampstand then does shine—
      Hallelujah, it is brightly shining now!

          Hallelujah for the Body!
          For the lampstands of the Body!
          For the golden, shining Body!
          Hallelujah, it is brightly shining now!

4   How may we express such oneness, be divine
        and shining too?
      Hallelujah, eating Jesus is the way!
     He's the tree of life, the manna, and the feast
        that's ever new—
      Hallelujah, we may eat Him every day!

          We are one by eating Jesus!
          We're divine by eating Jesus!
          How we shine by eating Jesus!
          Hallelujah, eating Jesus is the way!

Composition for prophecy with main point and sub-points: _____

_____
_____
_____
_____
_____
_____
_____
_____
_____
_____
_____
_____
_____
_____
_____
_____
_____
_____
_____
_____
_____
_____
_____
_____
_____
_____
_____
_____
_____
_____
_____
_____
_____
_____
_____
_____
_____
_____
_____

Reading Schedule for the Recovery Version of the Old Testament with Footnotes

Wk.	Lord's Day	Monday	Tuesday	Wednesday	Thursday	Friday	Saturday
1	Gen 1:1-5	1:6-23	1:24-31	2:1-9	2:10-25	3:1-13	3:14-24
2	4:1-26	5:1-32	6:1-22	7:1—8:3	8:4-22	9:1-29	10:1-32
3	11:1-32	12:1-20	13:1-18	14:1-24	15:1-21	16:1-16	17:1-27
4	18:1-33	19:1-38	20:1-18	21:1-34	22:1-24	23:1—24:27	24:28-67
5	25:1-34	26:1-35	27:1-46	28:1-22	29:1-35	30:1-43	31:1-55
6	32:1-32	33:1—34:31	35:1-29	36:1-43	37:1-36	38:1—39:23	40:1—41:13
7	41:14-57	42:1-38	43:1-34	44:1-34	45:1-28	46:1-34	47:1-31
8	48:1-22	49:1-15	49:16-33	50:1-26	Exo 1:1-22	2:1-25	3:1-22
9	4:1-31	5:1-23	6:1-30	7:1-25	8:1-32	9:1-35	10:1-29
10	11:1-10	12:1-14	12:15-36	12:37-51	13:1-22	14:1-31	15:1-27
11	16:1-36	17:1-16	18:1-27	19:1-25	20:1-26	21:1-36	22:1-31
12	23:1-33	24:1-18	25:1-22	25:23-40	26:1-14	26:15-37	27:1-21
13	28:1-21	28:22-43	29:1-21	29:22-46	30:1-10	30:11-38	31:1-17
14	31:18—32:35	33:1-23	34:1-35	35:1-35	36:1-38	37:1-29	38:1-31
15	39:1-43	40:1-38	Lev 1:1-17	2:1-16	3:1-17	4:1-35	5:1-19
16	6:1-30	7:1-38	8:1-36	9:1-24	10:1-20	11:1-47	12:1-8
17	13:1-28	13:29-59	14:1-18	14:19-32	14:33-57	15:1-33	16:1-17
18	16:18-34	17:1-16	18:1-30	19:1-37	20:1-27	21:1-24	22:1-33
19	23:1-22	23:23-44	24:1-23	25:1-23	25:24-55	26:1-24	26:25-46
20	27:1-34	Num 1:1-54	2:1-34	3:1-51	4:1-49	5:1-31	6:1-27
21	7:1-41	7:42-88	7:89—8:26	9:1-23	10:1-36	11:1-35	12:1—13:33
22	14:1-45	15:1-41	16:1-50	17:1—18:7	18:8-32	19:1-22	20:1-29
23	21:1-35	22:1-41	23:1-30	24:1-25	25:1-18	26:1-65	27:1-23
24	28:1-31	29:1-40	30:1—31:24	31:25-54	32:1-42	33:1-56	34:1-29
25	35:1-34	36:1-13	Deut 1:1-46	2:1-37	3:1-29	4:1-49	5:1-33
26	6:1—7:26	8:1-20	9:1-29	10:1-22	11:1-32	12:1-32	13:1—14:21

Reading Schedule for the Recovery Version of the Old Testament with Footnotes

Wk.	Lord's Day	Monday	Tuesday	Wednesday	Thursday	Friday	Saturday
27	14:22—15:23	16:1-22	17:1—18:8	18:9—19:21	20:1—21:17	21:18—22:30	23:1-25
28	24:1-22	25:1-19	26:1-19	27:1-26	28:1-68	29:1-29	30:1—31:29
29	31:30—32:52	33:1-29	34:1-12	Josh 1:1-18	2:1-24	3:1-17	4:1-24
30	5:1-15	6:1-27	7:1-26	8:1-35	9:1-27	10:1-43	11:1—12:24
31	13:1-33	14:1—15:63	16:1—18:28	19:1-51	20:1—21:45	22:1-34	23:1—24:33
32	Judg 1:1-36	2:1-23	3:1-31	4:1-24	5:1-31	6:1-40	7:1-25
33	8:1-35	9:1-57	10:1—11:40	12:1—13:25	14:1—15:20	16:1-31	17:1—18:31
34	19:1-30	20:1-48	21:1-25	Ruth 1:1-22	2:1-23	3:1-18	4:1-22
35	1 Sam 1:1-28	2:1-36	3:1—4:22	5:1—6:21	7:1—8:22	9:1-27	10:1—11:15
36	12:1—13:23	14:1-52	15:1-35	16:1-23	17:1-58	18:1-30	19:1-24
37	20:1-42	21:1—22:23	23:1—24:22	25:1-44	26:1-25	27:1—28:25	29:1—30:31
38	31:1-13	2 Sam 1:1-27	2:1-32	3:1-39	4:1—5:25	6:1-23	7:1-29
39	8:1—9:13	10:1—11:27	12:1-31	13:1-39	14:1-33	15:1—16:23	17:1—18:33
40	19:1-43	20:1—21:22	22:1-51	23:1-39	24:1-25	1 Kings 1:1-19	1:20-53
41	2:1-46	3:1-28	4:1-34	5:1—6:38	7:1-22	7:23-51	8:1-36
42	8:37-66	9:1-28	10:1-29	11:1-43	12:1-33	13:1-34	14:1-31
43	15:1-34	16:1—17:24	18:1-46	19:1-21	20:1-43	21:1—22:53	2 Kings 1:1-18
44	2:1—3:27	4:1-44	5:1—6:33	7:1-20	8:1-29	9:1-37	10:1-36
45	11:1—12:21	13:1—14:29	15:1-38	16:1-20	17:1-41	18:1-37	19:1-37
46	20:1—21:26	22:1-20	23:1-37	24:1—25:30	1 Chron 1:1-54	2:1—3:24	4:1—5:26
47	6:1-81	7:1-40	8:1-40	9:1-44	10:1—11:47	12:1-40	13:1—14:17
48	15:1—16:43	17:1-27	18:1—19:19	20:1—21:30	22:1—23:32	24:1—25:31	26:1-32
49	27:1-34	28:1—29:30	2 Chron 1:1-17	2:1—3:17	4:1—5:14	6:1-42	7:1—8:18
50	9:1—10:19	11:1—12:16	13:1—15:19	16:1—17:19	18:1—19:11	20:1-37	21:1—22:12
51	23:1—24:27	25:1—26:23	27:1—28:27	29:1-36	30:1—31:21	32:1-33	33:1—34:33
52	35:1—36:23	Ezra 1:1-11	2:1-70	3:1—4:24	5:1—6:22	7:1-28	8:1-36

Reading Schedule for the Recovery Version of the Old Testament with Footnotes

Wk.	Lord's Day	Monday	Tuesday	Wednesday	Thursday	Friday	Saturday
53	9:1—10:44	Neh 1:1-11	2:1—3:32	4:1—5:19	6:1-19	7:1-73	8:1-18
54	9:1-20	9:21-38	10:1—11:36	12:1-47	13:1-31	Esth 1:1-22	2:1—3:15
55	4:1—5:14	6:1—7:10	8:1-17	9:1—10:3	Job 1:1-22	2:1—3:26	4:1—5:27
56	6:1—7:21	8:1—9:35	10:1—11:20	12:1—13:28	14:1—15:35	16:1—17:16	18:1—19:29
57	20:1—21:34	22:1—23:17	24:1—25:6	26:1—27:23	28:1—29:25	30:1—31:40	32:1—33:33
58	34:1—35:16	36:1-33	37:1-24	38:1-41	39:1-30	40:1-24	41:1-34
59	42:1-17	Psa 1:1-6	2:1—3:8	4:1—6:10	7:1—8:9	9:1—10:18	11:1—15:5
60	16:1—17:15	18:1-50	19:1—21:13	22:1-31	23:1—24:10	25:1—27:14	28:1—30:12
61	31:1—32:11	33:1—34:22	35:1—36:12	37:1-40	38:1—39:13	40:1—41:13	42:1—43:5
62	44:1-26	45:1-17	46:1—48:14	49:1—50:23	51:1—52:9	53:1—55:23	56:1—58:11
63	59:1—61:8	62:1—64:10	65:1—67:7	68:1-35	69:1—70:5	71:1—72:20	73:1—74:23
64	75:1—77:20	78:1-72	79:1—81:16	82:1—84:12	85:1—87:7	88:1—89:52	90:1—91:16
65	92:1—94:23	95:1—97:12	98:1—101:8	102:1—103:22	104:1—105:45	106:1-48	107:1-43
66	108:1—109:31	110:1—112:10	113:1—115:18	116:1—118:29	119:1-32	119:33-72	119:73-120
67	119:121-176	120:1—124:8	125:1—128:6	129:1—132:18	133:1—135:21	136:1—138:8	139:1—140:13
68	141:1—144:15	145:1—147:20	148:1—150:6	Prov 1:1-33	2:1—3:35	4:1—5:23	6:1-35
69	7:1—8:36	9:1—10:32	11:1—12:28	13:1—14:35	15:1-33	16:1-33	17:1-28
70	18:1-24	19:1—20:30	21:1—22:29	23:1-35	24:1—25:28	26:1—27:27	28:1—29:27
71	30:1-33	31:1-31	Eccl 1:1-18	2:1—3:22	4:1—5:20	6:1—7:29	8:1—9:18
72	10:1—11:10	12:1-14	S.S 1:1-8	1:9-17	2:1-17	3:1-11	4:1-8
73	4:9-16	5:1-16	6:1-13	7:1-13	8:1-14	Isa 1:1-11	1:12-31
74	2:1-22	3:1-26	4:1-6	5:1-30	6:1-13	7:1-25	8:1-22
75	9:1-21	10:1-34	11:1—12:6	13:1-22	14:1-14	14:15-32	15:1—16:14
76	17:1—18:7	19:1-25	20:1—21:17	22:1-25	23:1-18	24:1-23	25:1-12
77	26:1-:21	27:1-13	28:1-29	29:1-24	30:1-33	31:1—32:20	33:1-24
78	34:1-17	35:1-10	36:1-22	37:1-38	38:1—39:8	40:1-31	41:1-29

Reading Schedule for the Recovery Version of the Old Testament with Footnotes

Wk.	Lord's Day	Monday	Tuesday	Wednesday	Thursday	Friday	Saturday
79	☐ 42:1-25	☐ 43:1-28	☐ 44:1-28	☐ 45:1-25	☐ 46:1-13	☐ 47:1-15	☐ 48:1-22
80	☐ 49:1-13	☐ 49:14-26	☐ 50:1—51:23	☐ 52:1-15	☐ 53:1-12	☐ 54:1-17	☐ 55:1-13
81	☐ 56:1-12	☐ 57:1-21	☐ 58:1-14	☐ 59:1-21	☐ 60:1-22	☐ 61:1-11	☐ 62:1-12
82	☐ 63:1-19	☐ 64:1-12	☐ 65:1-25	☐ 66:1-24	☐ Jer 1:1-19	☐ 2:1-19	☐ 2:20-37
83	☐ 3:1-25	☐ 4:1-31	☐ 5:1-31	☐ 6:1-30	☐ 7:1-34	☐ 8:1-22	☐ 9:1-26
84	☐ 10:1-25	☐ 11:1—12:17	☐ 13:1-27	☐ 14:1-22	☐ 15:1-21	☐ 16:1—17:27	☐ 18:1-23
85	☐ 19:1—20:18	☐ 21:1—22:30	☐ 23:1-40	☐ 24:1—25:38	☐ 26:1—27:22	☐ 28:1—29:32	☐ 30:1-24
86	☐ 31:1-23	☐ 31:24-40	☐ 32:1-44	☐ 33:1-26	☐ 34:1-22	☐ 35:1-19	☐ 36:1-32
87	☐ 37:1-21	☐ 38:1-28	☐ 39:1—40:16	☐ 41:1—42:22	☐ 43:1—44:30	☐ 45:1—46:28	☐ 47:1—48:16
88	☐ 48:17-47	☐ 49:1-22	☐ 49:23-39	☐ 50:1-27	☐ 50:28-46	☐ 51:1-27	☐ 51:28-64
89	☐ 52:1-34	☐ Lam 1:1-22	☐ 2:1-22	☐ 3:1-39	☐ 3:40-66	☐ 4:1-22	☐ 5:1-22
90	☐ Ezek 1:1-14	☐ 1:15-28	☐ 2:1—3:27	☐ 4:1—5:17	☐ 6:1—7:27	☐ 8:1—9:11	☐ 10:1—11:25
91	☐ 12:1—13:23	☐ 14:1—15:8	☐ 16:1-63	☐ 17:1—18:32	☐ 19:1-14	☐ 20:1-49	☐ 21:1-32
92	☐ 22:1-31	☐ 23:1-49	☐ 24:1-27	☐ 25:1—26:21	☐ 27:1-36	☐ 28:1-26	☐ 29:1—30:26
93	☐ 31:1—32:32	☐ 33:1-33	☐ 34:1-31	☐ 35:1—36:21	☐ 36:22-38	☐ 37:1-28	☐ 38:1—39:29
94	☐ 40:1-27	☐ 40:28-49	☐ 41:1-26	☐ 42:1—43:27	☐ 44:1-31	☐ 45:1-25	☐ 46:1-24
95	☐ 47:1-23	☐ 48:1-35	☐ Dan 1:1-21	☐ 2:1-30	☐ 2:31-49	☐ 3:1-30	☐ 4:1-37
96	☐ 5:1-31	☐ 6:1-28	☐ 7:1-12	☐ 7:13-28	☐ 8:1-27	☐ 9:1-27	☐ 10:1-21
97	☐ 11:1-22	☐ 11:23-45	☐ 12:1-13	☐ Hosea 1:1-11	☐ 2:1-23	☐ 3:1—4:19	☐ 5:1-15
98	☐ 6:1-11	☐ 7:1-16	☐ 8:1-14	☐ 9:1-17	☐ 10:1-15	☐ 11:1-12	☐ 12:1-14
99	☐ 13:1—14:9	☐ Joel 1:1-20	☐ 2:1-16	☐ 2:17-32	☐ 3:1-21	☐ Amos 1:1-15	☐ 2:1-16
100	☐ 3:1-15	☐ 4:1—5:27	☐ 6:1—7:17	☐ 8:1—9:15	☐ Obad 1-21	☐ Jonah 1:1-17	☐ 2:1—4:11
101	☐ Micah 1:1-16	☐ 2:1—3:12	☐ 4:1—5:15	☐ 6:1—7:20	☐ Nahum 1:1-15	☐ 2:1—3:19	☐ Hab 1:1-17
102	☐ 2:1-20	☐ 3:1-19	☐ Zeph 1:1-18	☐ 2:1-15	☐ 3:1-20	☐ Hag 1:1-15	☐ 2:1-23
103	☐ Zech 1:1-21	☐ 2:1-13	☐ 3:1-10	☐ 4:1-14	☐ 5:1—6:15	☐ 7:1—8:23	☐ 9:1-17
104	☐ 10:1—11:17	☐ 12:1—13:9	☐ 14:1-21	☐ Mal 1:1-14	☐ 2:1-17	☐ 3:1-18	☐ 4:1-6

Reading Schedule for the Recovery Version of the New Testament with Footnotes

Wk.	Lord's Day	Monday	Tuesday	Wednesday	Thursday	Friday	Saturday
1	Matt 1:1-2	1:3-7	1:8-17	1:18-25	2:1-23	3:1-6	3:7-17
2	4:1-11	4:12-25	5:1-4	5:5-12	5:13-20	5:21-26	5:27-48
3	6:1-8	6:9-18	6:19-34	7:1-12	7:13-29	8:1-13	8:14-22
4	8:23-34	9:1-13	9:14-17	9:18-34	9:35—10:5	10:6-25	10:26-42
5	11:1-15	11:16-30	12:1-14	12:15-32	12:33-42	12:43—13:2	13:3-12
6	13:13-30	13:31-43	13:44-58	14:1-13	14:14-21	14:22-36	15:1-20
7	15:21-31	15:32-39	16:1-12	16:13-20	16:21-28	17:1-13	17:14-27
8	18:1-14	18:15-22	18:23-35	19:1-15	19:16-30	20:1-16	20:17-34
9	21:1-11	21:12-22	21:23-32	21:33-46	22:1-22	22:23-33	22:34-46
10	23:1-12	23:13-39	24:1-14	24:15-31	24:32-51	25:1-13	25:14-30
11	25:31-46	26:1-16	26:17-35	26:36-46	26:47-64	26:65-75	27:1-26
12	27:27-44	27:45-56	27:57—28:15	28:16-20	Mark 1:1	1:2-6	1:7-13
13	1:14-28	1:29-45	2:1-12	2:13-28	3:1-19	3:20-35	4:1-25
14	4:26-41	5:1-20	5:21-43	6:1-29	6:30-56	7:1-23	7:24-37
15	8:1-26	8:27—9:1	9:2-29	9:30-50	10:1-16	10:17-34	10:35-52
16	11:1-16	11:17-33	12:1-27	12:28-44	13:1-13	13:14-37	14:1-26
17	14:27-52	14:53-72	15:1-15	15:16-47	16:1-8	16:9-20	Luke 1:1-4
18	1:5-25	1:26-46	1:47-56	1:57-80	2:1-8	2:9-20	2:21-39
19	2:40-52	3:1-20	3:21-38	4:1-13	4:14-30	4:31-44	5:1-26
20	5:27—6:16	6:17-38	6:39-49	7:1-17	7:18-23	7:24-35	7:36-50
21	8:1-15	8:16-25	8:26-39	8:40-56	9:1-17	9:18-26	9:27-36
22	9:37-50	9:51-62	10:1-11	10:12-24	10:25-37	10:38-42	11:1-13
23	11:14-26	11:27-36	11:37-54	12:1-12	12:13-21	12:22-34	12:35-48
24	12:49-59	13:1-9	13:10-17	13:18-30	13:31—14:6	14:7-14	14:15-24
25	14:25-35	15:1-10	15:11-21	15:22-32	16:1-13	16:14-22	16:23-31
26	17:1-19	17:20-37	18:1-14	18:15-30	18:31-43	19:1-10	19:11-27

Reading Schedule for the Recovery Version of the New Testament with Footnotes

Wk.	Lord's Day	Monday	Tuesday	Wednesday	Thursday	Friday	Saturday
27	Luke 19:28-48	20:1-19	20:20-38	20:39—21:4	21:5-27	21:28-38	22:1-20
28	22:21-38	22:39-54	22:55-71	23:1-43	23:44-56	24:1-12	24:13-35
29	24:36-53	John 1:1-13	1:14-18	1:19-34	1:35-51	2:1-11	2:12-22
30	2:23—3:13	3:14-21	3:22-36	4:1-14	4:15-26	4:27-42	4:43-54
31	5:1-16	5:17-30	5:31-47	6:1-15	6:16-31	6:32-51	6:52-71
32	7:1-9	7:10-24	7:25-36	7:37-52	7:53—8:11	8:12-27	8:28-44
33	8:45-59	9:1-13	9:14-34	9:35—10:9	10:10-30	10:31—11:4	11:5-22
34	11:23-40	11:41-57	12:1-11	12:12-24	12:25-36	12:37-50	13:1-11
35	13:12-30	13:31-38	14:1-6	14:7-20	14:21-31	15:1-11	15:12-27
36	16:1-15	16:16-33	17:1-5	17:6-13	17:14-24	17:25—18:11	18:12-27
37	18:28-40	19:1-16	19:17-30	19:31-42	20:1-13	20:14-18	20:19-22
38	20:23-31	21:1-14	21:15-22	21:23-25	Acts 1:1-8	1:9-14	1:15-26
39	2:1-13	2:14-21	2:22-36	2:37-41	2:42-47	3:1-18	3:19—4:22
40	4:23-37	5:1-16	5:17-32	5:33-42	6:1—7:1	7:2-29	7:30-60
41	8:1-13	8:14-25	8:26-40	9:1-19	9:20-43	10:1-16	10:17-33
42	10:34-48	11:1-18	11:19-30	12:1-25	13:1-12	13:13-43	13:44—14:5
43	14:6-28	15:1-12	15:13-34	15:35—16:5	16:6-18	16:19-40	17:1-18
44	17:19-34	18:1-17	18:18-28	19:1-20	19:21-41	20:1-12	20:13-38
45	21:1-14	21:15-26	21:27-40	22:1-21	22:22-29	22:30—23:11	23:12-15
46	23:16-30	23:31—24:21	24:22—25:5	25:6-27	26:1-13	26:14-32	27:1-26
47	27:27—28:10	28:11-22	28:23-31	Rom 1:1-2	1:3-7	1:8-17	1:18-25
48	1:26—2:10	2:11-29	3:1-20	3:21-31	4:1-12	4:13-25	5:1-11
49	5:12-17	5:18—6:5	6:6-11	6:12-23	7:1-12	7:13-25	8:1-2
50	8:3-6	8:7-13	8:14-25	8:26-39	9:1-18	9:19—10:3	10:4-15
51	10:16—11:10	11:11-22	11:23-36	12:1-3	12:4-21	13:1-14	14:1-12
52	14:13-23	15:1-13	15:14-33	16:1-5	16:6-24	16:25-27	1 Cor 1:1-4

Reading Schedule for the Recovery Version of the New Testament with Footnotes

Wk.	Lord's Day	Monday	Tuesday	Wednesday	Thursday	Friday	Saturday
53	1 Cor 1:5-9 ☐	1:10-17 ☐	1:18-31 ☐	2:1-5 ☐	2:6-10 ☐	2:11-16 ☐	3:1-9 ☐
54	3:10-13 ☐	3:14-23 ☐	4:1-9 ☐	4:10-21 ☐	5:1-13 ☐	6:1-11 ☐	6:12-20 ☐
55	7:1-16 ☐	7:17-24 ☐	7:25-40 ☐	8:1-13 ☐	9:1-15 ☐	9:16-27 ☐	10:1-4 ☐
56	10:5-13 ☐	10:14-33 ☐	11:1-6 ☐	11:7-16 ☐	11:17-26 ☐	11:27-34 ☐	12:1-11 ☐
57	12:12-22 ☐	12:23-31 ☐	13:1-13 ☐	14:1-12 ☐	14:13-25 ☐	14:26-33 ☐	14:34-40 ☐
58	15:1-19 ☐	15:20-28 ☐	15:29-34 ☐	15:35-49 ☐	15:50-58 ☐	16:1-9 ☐	16:10-24 ☐
59	2 Cor 1:1-4 ☐	1:5-14 ☐	1:15-22 ☐	1:23—2:11 ☐	2:12-17 ☐	3:1-6 ☐	3:7-11 ☐
60	3:12-18 ☐	4:1-6 ☐	4:7-12 ☐	4:13-18 ☐	5:1-8 ☐	5:9-15 ☐	5:16-21 ☐
61	6:1-13 ☐	6:14—7:4 ☐	7:5-16 ☐	8:1-15 ☐	8:16-24 ☐	9:1-15 ☐	10:1-6 ☐
62	10:7-18 ☐	11:1-15 ☐	11:16-33 ☐	12:1-10 ☐	12:11-21 ☐	13:1-10 ☐	13:11-14 ☐
63	Gal 1:1-5 ☐	1:6-14 ☐	1:15-24 ☐	2:1-13 ☐	2:14-21 ☐	3:1-4 ☐	3:5-14 ☐
64	3:15-22 ☐	3:23-29 ☐	4:1-7 ☐	4:8-20 ☐	4:21-31 ☐	5:1-12 ☐	5:13-21 ☐
65	5:22-26 ☐	6:1-10 ☐	6:11-15 ☐	6:16-18 ☐	Eph 1:1-3 ☐	1:4-6 ☐	1:7-10 ☐
66	1:11-14 ☐	1:15-18 ☐	1:19-23 ☐	2:1-5 ☐	2:6-10 ☐	2:11-14 ☐	2:15-18 ☐
67	2:19-22 ☐	3:1-7 ☐	3:8-13 ☐	3:14-18 ☐	3:19-21 ☐	4:1-4 ☐	4:5-10 ☐
68	4:11-16 ☐	4:17-24 ☐	4:25-32 ☐	5:1-10 ☐	5:11-21 ☐	5:22-26 ☐	5:27-33 ☐
69	6:1-9 ☐	6:10-14 ☐	6:15-18 ☐	6:19-24 ☐	Phil 1:1-7 ☐	1:8-18 ☐	1:19-26 ☐
70	1:27—2:4 ☐	2:5-11 ☐	2:12-16 ☐	2:17-30 ☐	3:1-6 ☐	3:7-11 ☐	3:12-16 ☐
71	3:17-21 ☐	4:1-9 ☐	4:10-23 ☐	Col 1:1-8 ☐	1:9-13 ☐	1:14-23 ☐	1:24-29 ☐
72	2:1-7 ☐	2:8-15 ☐	2:16-23 ☐	3:1-4 ☐	3:5-15 ☐	3:16-25 ☐	4:1-18 ☐
73	1 Thes 1:1-3 ☐	1:4-10 ☐	2:1-12 ☐	2:13—3:5 ☐	3:6-13 ☐	4:1-10 ☐	4:11—5:11 ☐
74	5:12-28 ☐	2 Thes 1:1-12 ☐	2:1-17 ☐	3:1-18 ☐	1 Tim 1:1-2 ☐	1:3-4 ☐	1:5-14 ☐
75	1:15-20 ☐	2:1-7 ☐	2:8-15 ☐	3:1-13 ☐	3:14—4:5 ☐	4:6-16 ☐	5:1-25 ☐
76	6:1-10 ☐	6:11-21 ☐	2 Tim 1:1-10 ☐	1:11-18 ☐	2:1-15 ☐	2:16-26 ☐	3:1-13 ☐
77	3:14—4:8 ☐	4:9-22 ☐	Titus 1:1-4 ☐	1:5-16 ☐	2:1-15 ☐	3:1-8 ☐	3:9-15 ☐
78	Philem 1:1-11 ☐	1:12-25 ☐	Heb 1:1-2 ☐	1:3-5 ☐	1:6-14 ☐	2:1-9 ☐	2:10-18 ☐

Reading Schedule for the Recovery Version of the New Testament with Footnotes

Wk.	Lord's Day	Monday	Tuesday	Wednesday	Thursday	Friday	Saturday
79	Heb 3:1-6	3:7-19	4:1-9	4:10-13	4:14-16	5:1-10	5:11—6:3
80	6:4-8	6:9-20	7:1-10	7:11-28	8:1-6	8:7-13	9:1-4
81	9:5-14	9:15-28	10:1-18	10:19-28	10:29-39	11:1-6	11:7-19
82	11:20-31	11:32-40	12:1-2	12:3-13	12:14-17	12:18-26	12:27-29
83	13:1-7	13:8-12	13:13-15	13:16-25	James 1:1-8	1:9-18	1:19-27
84	2:1-13	2:14-26	3:1-18	4:1-10	4:11-17	5:1-12	5:13-20
85	1 Pet 1:1-2	1:3-4	1:5	1:6-9	1:10-12	1:13-17	1:18-25
86	2:1-3	2:4-8	2:9-17	2:18-25	3:1-13	3:14-22	4:1-6
87	4:7-16	4:17-19	5:1-4	5:5-9	5:10-14	2 Pet 1:1-2	1:3-4
88	1:5-8	1:9-11	1:12-18	1:19-21	2:1-3	2:4-11	2:12-22
89	3:1-6	3:7-9	3:10-12	3:13-15	3:16	3:17-18	1 John 1:1-2
90	1:3-4	1:5	1:6	1:7	1:8-10	2:1-2	2:3-11
91	2:12-14	2:15-19	2:20-23	2:24-27	2:28-29	3:1-5	3:6-10
92	3:11-18	3:19-24	4:1-6	4:7-11	4:12-15	4:16—5:3	5:4-13
93	5:14-17	5:18-21	2 John 1:1-3	1:4-9	1:10-13	3 John 1:1-6	1:7-14
94	Jude 1:1-4	1:5-10	1:11-19	1:20-25	Rev 1:1-3	1:4-6	1:7-11
95	1:12-13	1:14-16	1:17-20	2:1-6	2:7	2:8-9	2:10-11
96	2:12-14	2:15-17	2:18-23	2:24-29	3:1-3	3:4-6	3:7-9
97	3:10-13	3:14-18	3:19-22	4:1-5	4:6-7	4:8-11	5:1-6
98	5:7-14	6:1-8	6:9-17	7:1-8	7:9-17	8:1-6	8:7-12
99	8:13—9:11	9:12-21	10:1-4	10:5-11	11:1-4	11:5-14	11:15-19
100	12:1-4	12:5-9	12:10-18	13:1-10	13:11-18	14:1-5	14:6-12
101	14:13-20	15:1-8	16:1-12	16:13-21	17:1-6	17:7-18	18:1-8
102	18:9—19:4	19:5-10	19:11-16	19:17-21	20:1-6	20:7-10	20:11-15
103	21:1	21:2	21:3-8	21:9-13	21:14-18	21:19-21	21:22-27
104	22:1	22:2	22:3-11	22:12-15	22:16-17	22:18-21	

Week 1 — Day 6   Today's verses

Psa. 45:13-17   The king's daughter is all glorious within *the royal abode*; her garment is a woven work inwrought with gold. She will be led to the King in embroidered *clothing*; the virgins behind her, her companions, will be brought to You. They will be led with rejoicing and exultation; they will enter the King's palace. In the place of Your fathers will be Your sons; You will make them princes in all the earth. I will cause Your name to be remembered in all generations; therefore the peoples will praise You forever and ever.

Date

Week 1 — Day 5   Today's verses

Psa. 45:9-12   The daughters of kings are among Your most prized; the queen stands at Your right hand in the gold of Ophir. Hear, O daughter, and see; and incline your ear; and forget your people and your father's house; thus the King will desire your beauty. Because He is your Lord, worship Him. And the daughter of Tyre *will come* with a gift; the rich among the people will entreat your favor.

Date

Week 1 — Day 4   Today's verses

Psa. 45:6-8   Your throne, O God, is forever and ever; the scepter of uprightness is the scepter of Your kingdom. You have loved righteousness and hated wickedness; therefore God, Your God, has anointed You with the oil of gladness above Your companions. All Your garments *smell* of myrrh and aloes, of cassia; from palaces of ivory, harpstrings have made You glad.

Date

Week 1 — Day 3   Today's verses

Psa. 45:2-5   You are fairer than the sons of men; grace is poured upon Your lips; therefore God has blessed You forever. Gird Your sword upon Your thigh, O mighty One, *in* Your majesty and Your splendor. And in Your splendor ride on victoriously because of truth and meekness *and* righteousness; and let Your right hand teach You awesome deeds. Your arrows are sharp: the peoples fall under You; *the arrows are in* the heart of the King's enemies.

Date

Week 1 — Day 2   Today's verses

Psa. 45 (title)   To the choir director: according to Shoshannim. Of the sons of Korah. A Maschil; a song of love.

1   My heart overflows with a good matter; I speak what I have composed concerning the King. My tongue is the pen of a ready writer.

Date

Week 1 — Day 1   Today's verses

John 1:14   And the Word became flesh and tabernacled among us (and we beheld His glory, glory as of the only Begotten from the Father), full of grace and reality.

1 Cor. 15:45   ...The last Adam *became* a life-giving Spirit.

Rev. 5:6   And I saw in the midst of the throne and of the four living creatures and in the midst of the elders a Lamb standing as having *just* been slain, having seven horns and seven eyes, which are the seven Spirits of God sent forth into all the earth.

2:7   He who has an ear, let him hear what the Spirit says to the churches. To him who overcomes, to him I will give to eat of the tree of life, which is in the Paradise of God.

Date

Week 2 — Day 4

Today's verses

Rev. And from Jesus Christ, the faithful Wit-
1:5 ness, the Firstborn of the dead, and the Ruler of the kings of the earth. To Him who loves us and has released us from our sins by His blood.

5:9 And they sing a new song, saying: You are worthy to take the scroll and to open its seals, for You were slain and have purchased for God by Your blood men out of every tribe and tongue and people and nation.

Gal. Christ has redeemed us out of the curse of
3:13 the law, having become a curse on our behalf; because it is written, "Cursed is everyone hanging on a tree."

Date

Week 2 — Day 5

Today's verses

Gal. In order that the blessing of Abraham
3:14 might come to the Gentiles in Christ Jesus, that we might receive the promise of the Spirit through faith.

4:4-5 But when the fullness of the time came, God sent forth His Son, born of a woman, born under law, that He might redeem those under law that we might receive the sonship.

Date

Week 2 — Day 6

Today's verses

1 Pet. Knowing that it was not with corruptible
1:18-19 things, with silver or gold, that you were redeemed from your vain manner of life handed down from your fathers, but with precious blood, as of a Lamb without blemish and without spot, the blood of Christ.

Titus Who gave Himself for us that He might
2:14 redeem us from all lawlessness and purify to Himself a particular people as His unique possession, zealous of good works.

Date

Week 2 — Day 1

Today's verses

1 Pet. ... The blood of Christ; who was
1:19-20 foreknown before the foundation of the world but has been manifested in the last of times for your sake.

Rom. Being justified freely by His grace through
3:24 the redemption which is in Christ Jesus.

1 Cor. For you have been bought with a price. So
6:20 then glorify God in your body.

Date

Week 2 — Day 2

Today's verses

Eph. To the praise of the glory of His grace,
1:6-7 with which He graced us in the Beloved; in whom we have redemption through His blood, the forgiveness of offenses, according to the riches of His grace.

Col. Who delivered us out of the authority of
1:13-14 darkness and transferred us into the kingdom of the Son of His love, in whom we have redemption, the forgiveness of sins.

Date

Week 2 — Day 3

Today's verses

Acts Take heed to yourselves and to all the
20:28 flock, among whom the Holy Spirit has placed you as overseers to shepherd the church of God, which He obtained through His own blood.

1 John But if we walk in the light as He is in the
1:7 light, we have fellowship with one another, and the blood of Jesus His Son cleanses us from every sin.

Heb. And not through the blood of goats and
9:12 calves but through His own blood, entered once for all into the Holy of Holies, obtaining an eternal redemption.

Date

Week 3 — Day 1

Today's verses

Exo. You also take the finest spices: of flowing
30:23-25 myrrh five hundred *shekels*, and of fragrant cinnamon half as much, two hundred fifty *shekels*, and of fragrant calamus two hundred fifty *shekels*, and of cassia five hundred *shekels*, according to the shekel of the sanctuary, and a hin of olive oil. And you shall make it a holy anointing oil, a fragrant ointment compounded according to the work of a compounder; it shall be a holy anointing oil.

1 Cor. ...The last Adam *became* a life-giving
15:45 Spirit.

_____
Date

Week 3 — Day 2

Today's verses

1 Cor. But if Christ is proclaimed that He has been
15:12-15 raised from the dead, how *is it that* some among you say that there is no resurrection of the dead? But if there is no resurrection of the dead, neither has Christ been raised. And if Christ has not been raised, then our proclamation is vain; your faith is vain also. And also we are found to be false witnesses of God because we have testified concerning God that He raised Christ, whom He did not raise, if indeed the dead are not raised.

58 Therefore, my beloved brothers, be steadfast, immovable, always abounding in the work of the Lord, knowing that your labor is not in vain in the Lord.

_____
Date

Week 3 — Day 3

Today's verses

Acts That God has fully fulfilled this *promise* to
13:33 us their children in raising up Jesus, as it is also written in the second Psalm, "You are My Son; this day have I begotten You."

_____
Date

Day ?

Today's verses

John But this He said concerning the Spirit,
7:39 whom those who believed into Him were about to receive; for *the* Spirit was not yet, because Jesus had not yet been glorified.

Phil. For I know that for me this will turn out to
1:19 salvation through your petition and *the* bountiful supply of the Spirit of Jesus Christ.

_____
Date

Week 3 — Day 5

Today's verses

1 Pet. Blessed be the God and Father of our Lord
1:3 Jesus Christ, who according to His great mercy has regenerated us unto a living hope through the resurrection of Jesus Christ from the dead.

1 Cor. For also in one Spirit we were all baptized
12:13 into one Body, whether Jews or Greeks, whether slaves or free, and were all given to drink one Spirit.

Week 3 — Day 6

Today's verses

Psa. Jehovah is my Shepherd; I will lack nothing.
23:1-2 He makes me lie down in green pastures; He leads me beside waters of rest.
3 He restores my soul; He guides me on the paths of righteousness for His name's sake.
4 Even though I walk through the valley of the shadow of death, I do not fear evil, for You are with me; Your rod and Your staff, they comfort me.
5 You spread a table before me in the presence of my adversaries; You anoint my head with oil; my cup runs over.
6 Surely goodness and lovingkindness will follow me all the days of my life, and I will dwell in the house of Jehovah for the length of *my* days.

_____
Date

Week 4 — Day 1

Today's verses

Rev. And in the midst of the lampstands One like
1:13-16 the Son of Man, clothed with a garment reaching to the feet, and girded about at the breasts with a golden girdle. And His head and hair were as white as white wool, as snow; and His eyes were like a flame of fire; and His feet were like shining bronze, as having been fired in a furnace; and His voice was like the sound of many waters. And He had in His right hand seven stars; and out of His mouth proceeded a sharp two-edged sword; and His face shone as the sun shines in its power.

3:1 ...These things says He who has the seven Spirits of God and the seven stars...

Date

Week 4 — Day 2

Today's verses

Rev. And out of the throne come forth
4:5 lightnings and voices and thunders. And there were seven lamps of fire burning before the throne, which are the seven Spirits of God.

5:6 And I saw in the midst of the throne...a Lamb standing as having just been slain, having seven horns and seven eyes, which are the seven Spirits of God sent forth into all the earth.

Date

Week 4 — Day 3

Today's verses

Rev. John to the seven churches which are in
1:4-5 Asia: Grace to you and peace from Him who is and who was and who is coming, and from the seven Spirits who are before His throne, and from Jesus Christ, the faithful Witness, the Firstborn of the dead, and the Ruler of the kings of the earth. To Him who loves us and has released us from our sins by His blood.

3:22 He who has an ear, let him hear what the Spirit says to the churches.

Date

Week 4 — Day 4

Today's verses

1 Pet. Beloved, do not think that the fiery ordeal
4:12 among you, coming to you for a trial, is strange, as if it were a strange thing happening to you.

17 For it is time for the judgment to begin from the house of God...

1:7 So that the proving of your faith, much more precious than of gold which perishes though it is proved by fire, may be found unto praise and glory and honor at the revelation of Jesus Christ.

Date

Week 4 — Day 5

Today's verses

Dan. I watched until thrones were set, and the
7:9-10 Ancient of Days sat down. His clothing was like white snow, and the hair of His head was like pure wool; His throne was flames of fire, its wheels, burning fire. A stream of fire issued forth and came out from before Him....

Rev. And he showed me a river of water of life,
22:1 bright as crystal, proceeding out of the throne of God and of the Lamb in the middle of its street.

Date

Week 4 — Day 6

Today's verses

Rom. And do not be fashioned according to this
12:2 age, but be transformed by the renewing of the mind that you may prove what the will of God is, that which is good and well pleasing and perfect.

8:29 Because those whom He foreknew, He also predestinated to be conformed to the image of His Son, that He might be the Firstborn among many brothers.

Rev. And I saw the holy city, New Jerusalem,
21:2 coming down out of heaven from God, prepared as a bride adorned for her husband.

Date

Week 5 — Day 6

Rev. And I saw...the Lamb standing on Mount
14:1 Zion, and with Him a hundred and forty-four thousand...
4 ...These are they who follow the Lamb wherever He may go. These were purchased from among men as firstfruits to God and to the Lamb.
15 And another angel came out of the temple, crying with a loud voice to Him who sat on the cloud, Send forth Your sickle and reap, for the hour to reap has come because the harvest of the earth is ripe.

Date

Week 5 — Day 3

Rev. But I have one thing against you, that you
2:4-5 have left your first love. Remember therefore where you have fallen from and repent and do the first works...
7 ...To him who overcomes, to him I will give to eat of the tree of life, which is in the Paradise of God.

Date

Rev. Saying, What you see write in a scroll and
1:11-12 send it to the seven churches: to Ephesus and to Smyrna and to Pergamos and to Thyatira and to Sardis and to Philadelphia and to Laodicea. And I turned to see the voice that spoke with me; and when I turned, I saw seven golden lampstands.

Date

Week 5 — Day 2

Rev. ...And there were seven lamps of fire
4:5 burning before the throne, which are the seven Spirits of God.
5:6 And I saw in the midst of the throne...a Lamb standing as having just been slain, having seven horns and seven eyes, which are the seven Spirits of God sent forth into all the earth.

Date

Rev. ...To him who overcomes, to him I will
2:17 give of the hidden manna, and to him I will give a white stone, and upon the stone a new name written, which no one knows except him who receives it.
3:5 He who overcomes will be clothed thus, in white garments, and I shall by no means erase his name out of the book of life, and I will confess his name before My Father and before His angels.

Date

Week 5 — Day 1

Rev. John to the seven churches which are in
1:4 Asia: Grace to you and peace from Him who is and who was and who is coming, and from the seven Spirits who are before His throne.
Psa. When I considered this in order to under-
73:16-17 stand it, it was a troublesome task in my sight, until I went into the sanctuary of God; then I perceived their end.

Date

Week 6 — Day 6

Exo. [The lampstand] shall be made of a talent
25:39 of pure gold, with all these utensils.
John God is Spirit, and those who worship Him
4:24 must worship in spirit and truthfulness.
20:22 And when He had said this, He breathed
into *them* and said to them, Receive the
Holy Spirit.

Date

Week 6 — Day 5

Today's verses

Exo. And you shall make a lampstand of pure
25:31 gold. The lampstand *with* its base and its
shaft shall be made of beaten work; its
cups, its calyxes, and its blossom buds
shall be of *one piece with* it.
36-37 Their calyxes and their branches shall be
of *one piece with* it; all of it one beaten
work of pure gold. And you shall make its
lamps, seven; and set up its lamps to give
light to the area in front of it.

Date

Week 6 — Day 4

2 Pet. ...That through these you might become
1:4 partakers of the divine nature....
Rev. And night will be no more; and they have
22:5 no need of the light of a lamp and of the
light of the sun, for the Lord God will
shine upon them; and they will reign forever and ever.
21:24 And the nations will walk by its light...

Date

Week 6 — Day 3

Today's verses

Rev. And I turned to see the voice that spoke
1:12 with me; and when I turned, I saw seven
golden lampstands.
21:18 And the building work of its wall was jasper; and the city was pure gold, like clear
glass.
23 And the city has no need of the sun or of
the moon that they should shine in it, for
the glory of God illumined it, and its lamp
is the Lamb.

Date

Week 6 — Day 2

Today's verses

Rev. ...What you see write in a scroll and send
1:11 *it* to the seven churches: to Ephesus and to
Smyrna and to Pergamos and to Thyatira
and to Sardis and to Philadelphia and to
Laodicea.
4:5 And out of the throne come forth
lightnings and voices and thunders. And
there were seven lamps of fire burning
before the throne, which are the seven
Spirits of God.
Dan. ...The people who know their God will
11:32 show strength and take action.

Date

Week 6 — Day 1

Today's verses

Rev. The mystery of the seven stars which you
1:20 saw upon My right hand and the seven
golden lampstands: The seven stars are
the messengers of the seven churches,
and the seven lampstands are the seven
churches.
21:2 And I saw the holy city, New Jerusalem,
coming down out of heaven from God,
prepared as a bride adorned for her husband.
Acts This One God has exalted to His right
5:31 hand as Leader and Savior, to give repentance to Israel and forgiveness of sins.

Date